A THYME TO DISCOVER

EARLY AMERICAN RECIPES FOR THE MODERN TABLE

TRICIA COHEN & LISA GRAVES
ILLUSTRATED BY LISA GRAVES

Skyhorse Publishing

Skyhorse Publishing books may be purchased in bulk at special discounts for sales promotion, corporate gifts, fund-raising, or educational purposes. Special editions can also be created to specifications. For details, contact the Special Sales Department, Skyhorse Publishing, 307 West 36th Street, 11th Floor, New York, NY 10018 or info@skyhorsepublishing.com.

Skyhorse® and Skyhorse Publishing® are registered trademarks of Skyhorse Publishing, Inc.®, a Delaware corporation.

Visit our website at www.skyhorsepublishing.com.

10 9 8 7 6 5 4 3 2

Library of Congress Cataloging-in-Publication Data is available on file.

Cover design by Jane Sheppard
Cover illustration by Lisa Graves

Print ISBN: 978-1-5107-2179-1
Ebook ISBN: 978-1-5107-2180-7

Printed in China

support *verb*/sə'pôrt/
1.   to endure bravely or quietly: bear
2.   to promote the interests or cause of: to uphold or defend as valid or right

This book is dedicated to Michael Cohen. His unwavering support and encouragement has made a difference in every aspect of our lives and in this book. Thank you, Michael.

Special thanks to:

Kathy Sandland, Sheila Graves, Jeanna Woods, Erin Beck, Colleen Bender, Christopher D'Addario, Edward Branley, Debbie and Adam Kessler, Joanna Huss, Sandy Tolliver, Sharon and Justin Coffini, Christine and Jerry Fellows, Michael Hill Kennedy II, Rebecca Guse, Raymond Bewsher, Michael King, Dr. Lois Frankel, and Kristen Flanagan.

Table of Contents

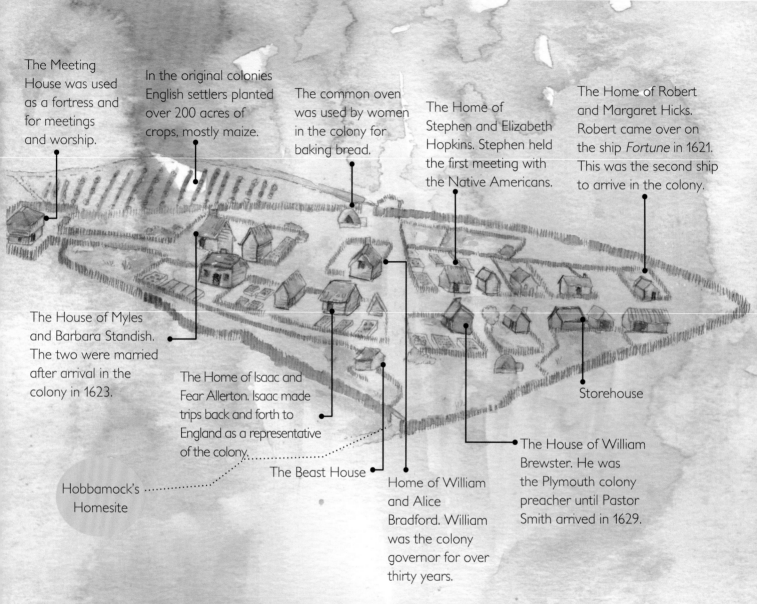

The Meeting House was used as a fortress and for meetings and worship.

In the original colonies English settlers planted over 200 acres of crops, mostly maize.

The common oven was used by women in the colony for baking bread.

The Home of Stephen and Elizabeth Hopkins. Stephen held the first meeting with the Native Americans.

The Home of Robert and Margaret Hicks. Robert came over on the ship *Fortune* in 1621. This was the second ship to arrive in the colony.

The House of Myles and Barbara Standish. The two were married after arrival in the colony in 1623.

The Home of Isaac and Fear Allerton. Isaac made trips back and forth to England as a representative of the colony.

Hobbamock's Homesite

The Beast House

Home of William and Alice Bradford. William was the colony governor for over thirty years.

Storehouse

The House of William Brewster. He was the Plymouth colony preacher until Pastor Smith arrived in 1629.

Hobbamock was a Native American that served as a guide and interpreter for the settlers in the colony. He was part of the Wampanoag tribe, and specifically asked by Massasoit to assist the Pilgrims. In Algonquian, Wampanoag translates to "People of the Dawn." He was a beloved friend of the settlers and was significantly instrumental to their survival.

Introduction

Picture yourself being dropped in the middle of the woods in a foreign country, with nothing but some salt, a couple of pots, and a few dishes. There is no Wi-Fi, everyone is sick, and you and your family have lived on nothing but rotting cardboard (or rather a substance that tastes like cardboard) for the past few months. Sounds like a reality horror show. Actually, it was a reality horror show.

Also throw in the fact that there are no grocery stores, you have no money, there's some very strange people lurking around the outskirts watching what you do, and you don't know how to hunt. When you really consider the circumstances the first settlers encountered once they reached the land we now know as *America* in 1620, it is amazing how any of them survived.

The land in Plimoth was plentiful, however. Chock full of native fruits and nuts, game birds filling the skies and forest, deer and game frolicking about, and the fish—oh, all the fish and clams and mussels and oysters! The problem was, no one knew how to hunt, fish, garden, or cook. The available ingredients were so foreign that no one knew if any of it was edible or how to prepare it, if it was.

Cooking a meal was incredibly taxing under these circumstances. Settlers would have to hunt, trap, pluck, farm, chop wood, harvest, etc., all while trying to build their village. Sure, things got better over the next thirty years with supplies coming in through the ports, but then after that you had the pesky Revolutionary War, the Salem witch trials, plagues, and religious turmoil.

Logistics and Lug Poles

In those first couple years, all the cooking was done in the hearth, which also served as the main source of light and heat in the house. Hearths were originally made of fieldstones, but they were eventually replaced by bricks. A lug pole was set over the fire to hang pots. At first, these poles were made of wood, but of course that caused them to burn easily, and they had to be replaced by iron rods. Most of the meals were a one-pot concoction—broth, meat, some vegetables, and herbs. This enabled the settlers to walk away from the hearth while it cooked to perform other household chores.

The Pilgrims who came over on the *Mayflower* were only allowed to bring minimal supplies due to storage space on the ship. This included one pot, one kettle, and a few platters/dishes/spoons. As a result, methods such as frying or poaching were very uncommon.

Dry goods were stored in baskets made of pine needles and corn husks and placed in the ground to keep cool. In fact, the settlers stole this technique from the Native Americans when they found a bunch of buried corn.

Farming was critical, but the settlers were not farmers. They had brought seeds with them, but it was difficult to clear land for crops. There was *so* much to be done. If they could have spent the entire day weeding, pruning, and caring for those crops, they would have certainly been more successful—the soil was rich, the conditions were manageable, and there was plenty of space. However, these people also needed to hunt, build their houses, make tools, and negotiate with the Native Americans, among many other tasks necessary for survival. Meals were merely a necessary break for fuel.

Influence and Influenza

The Columbian Exchange (named after the Italian explorer Christopher Columbus) was one of the most influential and significant events in the history of food. As settlers arrived in America and discovered new ways to sustain themselves, Europeans were experiencing the benefits as well of the cultural exchange as goods and supplies traveled between both continents. This resulted in a flourishing of new cuisines and dishes worldwide. Staples such as squash, pumpkins, turkeys, peanuts, potatoes, tomatoes, and corn made their way from their native America to Europe, Africa, and Asia; while grapes, bananas, coffee beans, olives, and livestock made their way to the Americas.

However, food was not the only thing that was exchanged. Unfortunately, this new ease of access resulted in the movement of deadly diseases and illnesses, such as smallpox, measles, and influenza, from the Old World to the New World, ultimately wiping out thousands of Native Americans. We might love our coffee, but a terrible price was paid for the cup of joe we drink today.

The Recipes

The colonial period is defined as the period from the arrival of the Europeans in 1492 up to the incorporation of the United States in 1776. That is *a lot* of time to cover during a period of radical change and population growth, which increased rapidly, practically at the speed of light! With this in mind, we have organized the history and recipes of the early Americans along a timeline, accompanied with mini chapters of interesting facts and information. We have researched historical recipes, available ingredients at the time, and old cooking methods, tools, and preparation techniques to create *modern* meals that you can cook and eat today. (We've done this to save you from going out into the woods and hunting, plucking, gathering, roasting, and potentially setting yourself on fire at a spit with a lug pole!) The recipes in this book are our interpretations of the information we have gathered.

Although we've included recipes inspired by Spanish settlers, Quakers, and Southern settlements, the majority of this book focuses on the New England area and its history. Perhaps it is because, as locals, we both grew up visiting Plimoth Plantation on every school field trip, or perhaps it is that we have great access to Boston, Newport, Plimoth, Sturbridge, and Cape Cod. Either way, we have tried to include a little something for everyone. This book is *not* a boring history lesson. Throughout the book, you will find bits and pieces of fascinating and funny facts about our American ancestors' cooking and eating habits that you can recite at the family dinner table or during a dinner party. For example, when serving our Fish House Punch (page 125), you'll be able to accuse your guests of being "halfway to Concord" after a few glasses; or perhaps you'll tell the story of "All Hail, Sarah Hale" at your next Thanksgiving feast (pages 34–35), giving thanks to her that you have the day off.

Enjoy!

The Mayflower made its first voyage in 1609, carrying a cargo from London to Norway. Along with several other trips to France, Germany, and Spain, it was primarily used for trade. In 1621, Master Christopher Jones was hired to take the ship on its first trip overseas to the New World. After its return in May of 1621, it was only used for a few more trips before being declared as in ruins in 1624. It is believed that it was dismantled and sold in pieces.

1620 to 1650s: A Time of Survival

The Arrival of the Pilgrims

QUICK! HIDE THE BEER

As one could imagine, the trip on the *Mayflower* was not exactly a high-end culinary experience. We will spare you the gruesome details of the food and not-so-fine dining conditions. Trust us, you do not want to hear about it.

The ship left England in September of 1620 and arrived in November that same year. On board were 102 passengers. One child was born during the trip and one passenger passed away. The group consisted of a mix of Separatists, indentured servants, and orphans looking to start anew in America. They were paid by The Virginia Company to establish a new British colony in Virginia, but that didn't go exactly as planned. The intention was to arrive in New York, but weather forced a landing in Cape Cod. Eventually, they made their way to Plimoth and dropped anchor on December 18, 1620.

The *Mayflower* captain and crew were eager to head back home to England and even more anxious to get the passengers away from the beer they were stockpiling for the return trip. As a result, the new colonists were forced to get the hell off the boat and figure out where to set up camp. Well, they ran out of beer anyway since, due to widespread illness, the *Mayflower* and its crew were unable to head back until April 5, 1621.

In the seventeenth century, words were spelled phonetically with many variations for the same word. Whereas the original spelling of *Plimoth* is with an "i," according to the history books, the modern spelling with a "y" was adapted to differentiate the Plimoth Plantation Museum from the town of Plymouth.

The passengers and crew made the most of what they had and choked down dishes such as:

Ship cakes or ship biscuits: large, round, hard biscuits made of flour and water
Dried peas
Ox tongue
Lobscouse: soup made with dried peas and salted beef
Burgoo: a boiled mix of hot oatmeal and molasses

Upon their arrival, they did discover mussels, but, uh, ate a little too much. We will leave it at that. We have put together a lovely, well-portioned mussel recipe for you instead.

WAIT . . . YOU CAN EAT THAT?

It is important to note that these people did not know how to survive in very foreign lands. The first few months were filled with harsh conditions, sickness, food shortages, fear of Native American attacks, and lack of resources, tools, and hunting skills. Foods that were native to the land were difficult to understand and prepare as the Pilgrims had never seen them before. This included corn; pumpkins; squash; various nuts, herbs, and berries; as well as venison and . . . mussels.

Pea and Mint Soup

Vibrant and fresh, this is a much better version than what they would have served on the Mayflower.

INGREDIENTS

1½ Tbsp olive oil
2 Tbsp unsalted butter
2 cloves garlic, minced
2 cups leeks (white portion only), cleaned, trimmed, and sliced
⅓ cup all-purpose flour
4 cups vegetable stock
39 oz young peas (about 3 bags), thawed and drained
6 oz baby spinach
⅓ cup mint leaves, chopped
Zest, 1 lemon
Juice, 1 lemon
½ tsp white pepper
1 tsp salt
1 small container crème fraiche
1 tsp ground coriander

DIRECTIONS

- Heat the oil and butter in a Dutch oven over medium heat. Add the garlic and leeks, cooking until they soften.

- Add the flour, and stir continuously for 2 minutes. Be careful not to let the flour burn.

- Pour a small amount of the stock into the Dutch oven, and stir to prevent lumps. Add the rest of the stock and raise the heat to medium-high. Once the soup starts to boil, add the peas, spinach, and mint leaves. Lower the heat to simmer. Add the lemon zest and juice.

- Cook until the spinach wilts and the peas are soft. Remove from heat and cool slightly.

- Add soup to a blender, in batches, to blend and puree the vegetables. Strain the pureed soup through a sieve and pour it back into the Dutch oven.

- Turn the heat to low, and add the pepper, salt, crème fraiche, and coriander. Simmer for 20 minutes. Serve.

Ship Legs Need Mussels~and Beer

Mussels drowning in beer and herbs.

INGREDIENTS

2 lb mussels
6 Tbsp unsalted butter, divided
4 cloves garlic, minced
2 large shallots, thinly sliced
8 oz Belgian beer (we used Stella Artois)
1 Tbsp fresh chervil, finely chopped
2 Tbsp fresh chives, finely chopped
¼ cup fresh flat leaf parsley, finely chopped
¼ cup Madeira wine
Brioche bread, for dipping

TIP

To sop up your broth, you can also use Skillet Flatbread (page 18) for dipping, a modernized version of ship cakes (you really don't want the original recipe).

DIRECTIONS

- Rinse and stir mussels under cold, running, fresh water. For any mussels that do not close after rinsing, tap their shells or lightly squeeze them while running under the water again. For any mussel that still does not close, throw it away—this is a sign that it is not safe to eat.

- Melt 2 Tbsp unsalted butter in a deep pan, on medium heat. Add garlic and cook until fragrant. Add shallots, and cook until translucent. Watch the shallots to ensure they do not burn.

- Add the mussels, and then pour beer over the mussels. Stir to coat and cover with a lid. Turn the heat up to medium-high for 5–7 minutes. Shake the pan periodically to move the mussels around instead of opening the lid and releasing the steam. When the mussels are open, you are ready to proceed.

- Remove the lid, and lower the heat to medium. Add the remaining 4 Tbsp butter and herbs. Stir to ensure that all the mussels have been coated with butter and herbs. Remove the mussels with a slotted spoon and place in a deep bowl. Lightly tent with aluminum foil. Keep the juices in the pan.

- Turn the heat up to medium-high. Add the Madeira wine. Stir and cook the sauce down for 3 minutes. Remove the pan from the heat. Remove the aluminum foil from the mussels. Pour the sauce from the pan over the mussels.

- Toast slices of brioche and cut into triangles. Arrange the triangles around the mussel bowl for proper dipping.

Skillet Flatbread

This simple name is perfect for how easy this recipe is. Do you ever find yourself in a position when you are short of a bread item for dinner or an impromptu guest? This simple flatbread uses common ingredients, can be whipped up in 20 minutes, and is versatile.

INGREDIENTS

1 cup self-rising flour
½ tsp baking powder
1 tsp salt
3 Tbsp plain Greek yogurt
2½ Tbsp canola or vegetable oil
2–4 Tbsp water, lukewarm
Lard (or whatever cooking fat you choose to use)

Optional topping:
½ stick unsalted butter
2 tsp fresh rosemary, minced
3 cloves garlic, minced
Flaked salt, to sprinkle

DIRECTIONS

* Combine the flour, baking powder, and salt in a large mixing bowl. Add the Greek yogurt and oil, and combine (use the back of a wooden spoon to help). Add the water until the dough is able to come together and has the ability to be rolled into a ball with your hands. The dough should stick together, and be lightly tacky. The appearance will not look silky and smooth like bread dough, so don't panic if it looks rough. Wrap the ball with plastic wrap and pop in the refrigerator for 10 minutes at least.

* Remove chilled dough and place on a lightly floured surface. Slice the dough in half (the dough makes 2 flatbreads). Using your hands or a rolling pin, stretch and flatten the first piece of dough. We prefer to keep it ¼- to ½-inch thick—the thinner the dough the crunchier it is, and we like it a little less crunchy.

* Heat a cast-iron pan on medium-high heat. Add lard (or butter or oil). Lard cooks at a high temperature, does not burn very easily, and provides a subtle flavor. Once the pan is hot and the lard has melted and warmed, gently place one of the dough rounds in the pan. If your pan is really hot, it should take no more than 2 minutes to get golden brown in spots, or a little longer if you are cooking at a lower temperature. Flip the dough over and cook the other side.

* Optional topping: Melt the butter in a saucepan, and add rosemary and garlic. When the dough is cooked, brush this butter mix on top and sprinkle with flaked salt.

Lobscouse

This classic stew has been a traditional sailor's meal for hundreds of years. Hearty and full of flavor, our version will delight all those on land and sea.

INGREDIENTS

½ cup all-purpose flour
1 tsp salt
2 tsp pepper, divided
2 lb stew meat, cut into 1-inch pieces (we used beef chuck)
4 Tbsp butter, unsalted
5 cups chicken stock
1 bottle of Belgian beer (we used Stella Artois)
2 potatoes, peeled and cubed (we used russet potatoes)
1½ cup carrots, sliced
2 bay leaves
2 soup bones*
1 Tbsp Worcestershire sauce

DIRECTIONS

→ In a plastic bag, mix flour, salt, and 1 tsp pepper. Add meat in batches until all the meat is covered with the flour. Discard the bag of flour.

→ Heat butter in a Dutch oven, over medium heat. Working in batches, brown the meat and then remove. Set aside.

→ Pour 1 cup chicken stock into the pan. Using a wooden spoon, stir up all the browned bits at the bottom of the pan. Pour remaining chicken stock and beer into pan, and stir. Raise the heat to medium-high to get the liquid to boil. Return the meat to the pan, along with the potatoes, carrots, bay leaves, soup bones, and Worcestershire sauce. Stir, and add remaining 1 tsp pepper.

→ Lower the temperature to simmer. Cook for 2 hours. About an hour into the cooking process, use a butter knife to loosen the marrow out of the soup bones so it will melt into the soup. Soup bones are often a forgotten ingredient that, when included, add depth of flavor.

→ Remove bay leaves and soup bones; discard. As always, soup tastes better the next day, but this is certainly delicious on the first day as well. Suggestion: serve with Skillet Flatbread (page 20).

*TIP

Ahhh, soup bones. We know you are thinking, *What is that?* Instead, you should be thinking, *Why haven't I used this ingredient before?* Soup bones are a tremendous addition to your soups, stews, or favorite pasta sauces. Soups, specifically liquids, extract the amazing flavor from bones and marrow, enriching the dish. This quick, inexpensive ingredient can add so much with very little effort. Generally, you can find marrow-rich bones in the same grocery aisle that you purchase your meat. If you are lucky enough to have a butcher in your community, they can also accommodate you.

The Harvest of 1621

Or, as We Call It, the First Thanksgiving

The Wampanoag Tribe or "People of the First Light" were a peaceful but cautious group. Their leader, Massasoit, met with the colonists on a few occasions to discuss a way everyone could live and learn from each other. This peaceful union led to a gathering in 1621. Massasoit was invited to celebrate the successful and bountiful harvest (which would have *never* happened without the help of the Wampanoags). He accepted the invitation and brought ninety men with him. Women and children were sent for later, after it was determined that there was no threat or danger. However, the colonists did not plan on having so many guests and were quite short on supplies for the visitors. Massasoit commanded his best hunters to go out immediately and bring back the needed venison and other game to supplement the feast.

Preparing the food was incredibly labor-intensive (no pre-cut meats wrapped in plastic), but everyone participated and helped with the butchering, plucking, grinding, shucking, roasting, and serving. It was truly a collaborative effort.

The feast went on for three days—not just a single meal, as we have today, but many. They did not just eat and drink; there were also talks of diplomacy, military drills, games, and various types of entertainment. A good time was had by all. The Wampanoags were and still are a people with a strong sense of community and family, so one could guess that this was, indeed, celebratory and inclusive.

Although the modern-day observation of Thanksgiving involves one large meal with family and a traditional menu, this first feast was not filled with turkey, mashed potatoes, and cranberry sauce. Instead, food included eels, clams, oysters, cod, sea bass, wild onions, leeks, watercress, duck, geese, venison, dried plums, berries, beans, squash, nuts, wine, and, of course, cornmeal. Just rewards for a year of hard work.

It is a shame that after all this diplomacy, shared knowledge, and peace, a full-scale war developed in 1675 between the natives and the English known as King Philip's War.

The Wampanoag Tribe

The Wampanoag Tribe held territory from Rhode Island up through Massachusetts, inland and coastal, as well as on Martha's Vineyard and Nantucket. Roughly sixty-five villages were scattered throughout New England in the early seventeenth century.

In 1615, the first of several epidemics swept through their villages; it is suspected to have been smallpox or a bacterial infection. The epidemic destroyed families and wiped out entire villages, bringing their numbers down from about 40,000 to about 6,000. As a result, having an alliance with the colonists became imperative to hold their territories and protect themselves from other Native American tribes.

They often cooked in clay pots, and they utilized everything nature provided. Dishes such as *nasaump* (porridge) are still made today according to tradition, using berries, nuts, acorns, and chestnuts to create a flavorful meal. Other dishes included *sobaheg* (stew), *marachock* (passion flower) jelly, *msiekquatash* (succotash), *sautauthig* (blueberry cornmeal porridge), and *puttuckqunnege* (boiled bread).

Hobbamock, or Squanto, was instrumental in the survival of the colonists. With his fluent English, sense of diplomacy, and farming and hunting skills, we modern Americans all owe him a beer or two.

Today, the Wampanoags continue traditions from their early days—storytelling, reviving their language, organizing internal governments, and maintaining respect for nature through ceremonies, dance, and cooking. They have adapted to modern techniques, while passing on the story of their heritage.

Massasoit, the Grand Sachem

Massasoit, along with Samoset and Squanto, is credited for saving the American colonists from certain starvation. He was born in 1590 near what is now known as Bristol, Rhode Island. He was the Grand Sachem, or leader, of the Wampanoag Indians.

Samoset, a subordinate chief, convinced Massasoit that a peaceful alliance with the new colonists would benefit the tribe and protect their territories. Massasoit agreed, and so began a peaceful union. This alliance lasted until shortly after his death in 1661. During the peaceful years, Massasoit shared knowledge and techniques that the settlers were in desperate need of. In return, along with the feast of 1621, the colonists were instrumental in nursing the Grand Sachem back to health in 1623 after a bout of dangerous illness.

There is not a lot of information available about his personal life, but we do know he had five children. He was described as being a man of few words, but when he spoke, you listened!

After his death, more settlers arrived, causing tension as resources were depleted and settlers demanded more land. This all led to a very bloody battle led by Massasoit's second son, Metacomet (who later became King Philip). King Philip's War was one of the deadliest battles in US history, lasting for one year.

Steamed Pumpkin Pudding with Rum Hard Sauce

Don't be confused by the name pudding, *which is the traditional name or description for any cake that is steamed, baked, or boiled. This is an incredible moist cake that can be consumed warm or cold, for breakfast or dessert. Or in one sitting . . .*

INGREDIENTS

Pumpkin Pudding:

8 Tbsp unsalted butter, room temperature (plus extra to prepare the pan)
1 cup brown sugar, packed
2 large eggs
¾ cup pumpkin puree
¼ tsp cloves
1¾ cups all-purpose flour
½ tsp salt
1 tsp baking soda
½ tsp cinnamon
½ tsp ground ginger
¼ tsp nutmeg
½ cup buttermilk

Rum Hard Sauce:

4 Tbsp unsalted butter, room temperature
¾ cup confectioners' sugar
Pinch nutmeg
3 tsp spiced rum

DIRECTIONS

Pumpkin Pudding:

- Set the oven to 350 degrees. Butter a Bundt pan or ring mold with the extra butter.

- In a mixing bowl, add 8 Tbsp butter and whip until light. Add the sugar, followed by the eggs, one at a time. You may need to scrape the side of the bowl down before the next step. Now, mix in the pumpkin puree and cloves.

- In a medium size bowl, combine the flour, salt, baking soda, cinnamon, ginger, and ¼ tsp nutmeg.

- Have your buttermilk ready for the next step. In the mixing bowl with the butter and pumpkin mixture, alternate adding in the dry mixture with the buttermilk three times, while the mixer is on a low speed. We recommend scraping down the sides at least once.

- Add the batter to your prepared pan. Seal the top tightly with aluminum foil. Cook in the oven for 1 hour.

Rum Hard Sauce:

- Add 4 Tbsp butter to a mixing bowl and whip until light. Shut off the mixer and add the confectioners' sugar. Turn the mixer back on slowly. Once the ingredients are fully combined, mix in the pinch of nutmeg and rum.

- When the cake is done, remove from the oven and let cool. Remove the foil. As the cake cools, it will pull away from the sides of the pan, allowing you to easily release the cake from the pan when you invert it over a plate.

- Pour Rum Hard Sauce over the top of the warm cake, or on the side, and serve.

Maple and Herbs Acorn Squash

An easy and impressive Thanksgiving side dish.

INGREDIENTS

1 acorn squash*
Olive oil, for brushing
1 Tbsp apple cider vinegar
5 Tbsp sliced almonds
1 tsp salt
1 tsp pepper
3 Tbsp honey
3 Tbsp maple syrup
1 tsp cinnamon
2 Tbsp unsalted butter
2 tsp fresh thyme

DIRECTIONS

- Preheat oven at 400 degrees.

- Brush the flesh of the squash with olive oil, and roast in the oven for 15 minutes.

- Combine the remaining ingredients in a saucepan on medium heat. Cook until the butter has melted and the ingredients thicken.

- Pour the mixture into the wells of the squash.

- Cook the squash for another 25–30 minutes or until the squash is soft.

- Serve warm.

*TIP

Cut the squash in half, and remove and discard any seeds. Eventually, you will be filling the well of the squash, so you will want to ensure that it sits flat in a roasting pan. We trimmed off a portion from the bottom of the squash to achieve that goal. Acorn squash has a thin, delicate, and edible skin; therefore, you do not need to peel it.

Pawpaw-ish Cookies with Maple Glaze

Pawpaw is a fruit similar in taste to bananas. Pawpaw were grown wild and consumed by Native Americans.

INGREDIENTS

Cookies:
1½ cups ripe bananas, mashed
¾ cup unsalted butter, room temperature
¾ cup brown sugar, packed
1 large egg
1 tsp maple syrup extract
2 cups all-purpose flour
¼ tsp salt
1 tsp baking soda
⅛ tsp nutmeg
½ tsp cinnamon
¼ tsp ground cardamom

Glaze:
½ cup unsalted butter, melted
6 Tbsp brown sugar, packed
4 Tbsp cream (or whole milk)
1 tsp maple syrup extract
3 cups confectioners' sugar

DIRECTIONS

Cookies:

- Set the oven temperature to 350 degrees. Add bananas to a blender and puree. Set aside.

- Whip butter in a mixer. Add brown sugar and continue to beat until fully incorporated. While the mixer is going, add the egg, followed by the maple syrup extract.

- In a separate bowl, combine the flour, salt, baking soda, and spices.

- Lower the mixer speed, and alternate adding the banana and flour mix, scraping the sides down while you do so. Repeat these steps two additional times until the butter and flour are fully combined.

- Scoop a spoonful of the batter onto a lined cookie sheet. Do not overcrowd the pan as the mixture will spread and puff up. Cook for 12 to 14 minutes in the oven.

Glaze:

- While the cookies are baking, prepare the glaze. Combine the butter and brown sugar in a mixing bowl. Add the cream and maple syrup extract, and stir. Add the confectioners' sugar to the mixing bowl, and blend until fully combined.

- Remove the cookies from the oven, and spoon the glaze over the warm cookie. Let cool and watch them disappear.

Venison with Blackberry Sauce Over Wild Rice Cakes

Venison, when prepared correctly, can taste like the most tender piece of meat. Purchasing venison from a fine purveyor is a necessary part of the process. We know that you all have a great "Uncle Leo" who is an avid hunter; however, just because he is an awesome uncle doesn't mean he is the best butcher. Venison that is not processed properly will taste gamy and can be almost inedible. If you have never tried venison, spend the few extra dollars to purchase the meat from purveyors like D'Artagnan (D'Artagnan prepares and packages meat in a way that removes the "gaminess" from the taste). It will change the way you view venison.

INGREDIENTS

Venison:
2 tenderloins, trimmed
Buttermilk
4 Tbsp unsalted butter, divided
2 Tbsp shallot, minced
5 cloves garlic (2 cloves minced, 3 cloves smashed)
1½ cups wild mushrooms mixture (use more earthy-tasting mushrooms, like morel and oyster, to complement the meat and balance the flavor)
Rosemary; 1 tsp minced, 2–3 sprigs whole
¾ tsp salt, divided
¾ tsp pepper, divided
4 Tbsp chicken stock
1 cup baby spinach
12 juniper berries

Blackberry Sauce:
5 Tbsp butter, unsalted, divided
¼ cup shallots, thinly sliced
2 cloves garlic, minced
⅔ cup chicken stock
⅔ cup Cabernet Sauvignon
3 Tbsp balsamic vinegar
3 Tbsp brown sugar, packed
1 Tbsp sage, minced
¼ tsp salt
¼ tsp white pepper
2 cups blackberries, rinsed

DIRECTIONS

Venison:

➤ Place the tenderloins in a shallow container. Cover the meat completely in buttermilk, moving the meat around to ensure that the buttermilk is covering all sides of the meat. Cover, and place the meat in the refrigerator until you are ready to use it, for at least 1 hour. The buttermilk will draw out any "gamy" taste from the meat.

➤ Add 2 Tbsp butter to a sauté pan on medium heat. Add shallots and 2 cloves minced garlic until they start to soften but not brown. Add the mushrooms, minced rosemary, ¼ tsp salt, and ¼ tsp pepper to the pan, and sauté until the liquid has evaporated. Add the chicken stock and spinach, and cook down until the liquid is gone, but not so much that the spinach sticks to the pan (in other words, watch the pan!). Remove the sauté pan from the stovetop and set aside.

→ Remove the tenderloins from the refrigerator. Lightly rinse the buttermilk from the meat, and discard the buttermilk. Pat the tenderloins dry with a paper towel.

→ Using a mortar and pestle, combine the remaining salt and pepper (½ tsp each) along with the juniper berries. Grind down until a powder forms.

→ Lay the meat on a flat surface. Using a sharp knife, cut a slice in the side of the meat from almost one end to another, creating a pocket. Take your time with this step. You want to create a deep pocket, but you do not want to cut straight through to the other side.

→ Stuff each pocket with the mushroom and spinach mixture. Using cooking twine, tress the meat to prevent the stuffing from falling out. Some of the stuffing may come out, and that is fine, but the twine should prevent most of it from falling out. After the meat is tied up, rub the juniper powder all over both pieces, and set the meat aside for a few minutes to bring to room temperature.

→ Set the oven temperature to 375 degrees.

→ Place a cast-iron pan on the stovetop and heat on medium-high. Once the pan is hot, add the remaining 2 Tbsp butter to the pan. Carefully place each piece of tenderloin in the pan, followed by 2–3 whole rosemary sprigs and 3 cloves smashed garlic. The rosemary and garlic will infuse with the butter, adding another layer of flavor. Cook the meat until it browns, just a few minutes, and then flip over to the other side. Immediately transfer the cast-iron pan to the oven and cook for 10 minutes. Medium-rare is the recommended temperature.

→ Remove the meat from the pan and let it rest for at least 5 minutes before cutting. Remove the strings, and slice the meat into 1-inch slices.

Blackberry Sauce:

→ In a saucepan, melt 1 Tbsp butter on medium heat. Add the shallots and garlic, cooking until soft but not brown.

→ Add the chicken stock and wine, reducing it down to 3 Tbsp of liquid.

→ Add the balsamic vinegar, brown sugar, sage, salt, and pepper. Mix well. Now add the blackberries into the sauce, stir, and cook for about 8 minutes. You will see that the blackberries start to get plump.

→ Remove the pan from the heat, and strain through a sieve. Tap the sieve to make sure you captured all the liquid. Put the silky liquid back in the pan (discard the solids), heat on medium, and slowly add the remaining 4 Tbsp butter with a whisk.

→ Serve with the venison. The flavor will have a slight bitterness, but when paired with the venison, it balances perfectly. Serve with the Wild Rice Cakes (page 30).

INGREDIENTS

Wild Rice Cakes

1 cup wild rice (we used a blend of white, brown, wild, and red rice)
1½ cups vegetable stock
2½ Tbsp unsalted butter, divided
1 tsp salt (we used black truffle salt), divided
3 cloves garlic, minced
1 cup leeks, trimmed, cored, cleaned, and minced
1 cup raw carrots, shredded
¾ cup shiitake mushrooms, sliced
¼ cup oyster mushrooms, diced
½ tsp white pepper
1 tsp baking powder
1/3 cup flour, plus 2 Tbsp, divided
2 large eggs, whisked
1½ cups panko
Olive oil

DIRECTIONS

Wild Rice Cakes:

➷ In a small stockpot, combine rice, stock, 1 Tbsp butter, and ½ tsp salt on medium-high heat. Once the liquid starts to boil, drop the heat to simmer, cover, and cook for 15 minutes. Remove from heat and set aside for 10 minutes. The rice will continue to cook.

➷ Melt 1 Tbsp butter in a small sauté pan. Add garlic and leeks. Cook until tender and remove from the heat. Add the cooked leek mixture, and the raw carrots, to a large mixing bowl, and set aside.

➷ Wipe sauté pan with a paper towel, melt ½ Tbsp butter in pan, and add mushrooms. Cook until tender and until there is no liquid in pan. Add mushrooms to the mixing bowl with the other vegetables.

➷ Once all the vegetables have cooled, add ½ tsp salt, white pepper, baking powder, 1/3 cup flour, and whisked eggs. The mixture should still be wet but able to be held together. Sometimes the vegetables provide additional moisture, so to be able to make this into a patty you may need to add up to 2 additional Tbsp flour.

➷ Place the panko in a shallow plate and set aside. Scoop enough mixture into your hands to cover your palm. Shape and flatten until it resembles the size of a crab cake. Gently press the patty into the panko, on all sides. Place the patty on a lined cookie sheet, and repeat until all the mixture is used. Depending on the size, this will make 8 patties. Cover and place in refrigerator for a minimum of 1 hour.

➷ Add a layer of olive oil in a large frying pan. Warm the pan on medium heat. Add the rice cakes to the pan and cook each side until they brown.

➷ We had to make these twice because we ate the first batch. This is great as a main dinner item, as a base for our Venison with Blackberry Sauce (page 28), or as a small plate.

Sun-Roasted Clams in the Sand

AKA oven-roasted clams in breadcrumbs.

INGREDIENTS

2 dozen littleneck clams
Cornmeal
3 Tbsp butter, unsalted
2 shallots, minced
3 cloves garlic, minced
1 lemon, zest and juice (about 5 Tbsp)
½ cup white wine (we used Sauvignon Blanc)
12 basil leaves, rolled up and sliced into strips
¾ tsp salt
½ tsp white pepper
1½ cups plain breadcrumbs

DIRECTIONS

→ The first thing you always do with clams is inspect and clean. Immediately throw out any clams that are already open. Add the clams to a large bowl of cold tap water, with a heavy sprinkle of cornmeal, and leave for 20 minutes. The cornmeal will encourage the clams to expel any sand that is hiding in the shell.

→ Preheat the oven to 350 degrees. On the stovetop, melt the butter on medium heat. Add the shallots, garlic, and lemon zest first. Do not brown; just lightly sauté. Add the lemon juice, white wine, basil, salt, and pepper. Reduce heat slightly.

→ Rinse the clams and lay them in a roasting pan. Pop the pan in the oven and cook until the clams have all opened. This should take anywhere from 8–12 minutes, but do not give up if they have not all opened yet. Remove the ones that have opened (be careful not to lose the juice inside the shell), and continue to cook the rest for a few more minutes to see if they open. If they do not open, throw them out.

→ Lower the heat on the stove to low. Add the breadcrumbs to the wine mixture, and stir until the breadcrumbs fully absorb the liquid.

→ Add the clams, along with their juice, into the sauté pan. Stir and serve. Add a few more thin ribbons of basil and a few wedges of lemons, if you so choose.

Pan-Seared Duck Breast with Herbed Blueberry Drizzle

You may want to do more than drizzle that sauce over your duck . . .

INGREDIENTS

¾ tsp whole anise seed
5 whole juniper berries
¾ tsp salt
½ tsp pepper
1 lb duck breast
¼ cup balsamic vinegar
1 cup Madeira wine
1 cup chicken stock
⅓ cup brown sugar, packed
2 tsp rosemary, minced
2 cups blueberries
4 Tbsp unsalted butter, cut into 4 pieces

DIRECTIONS

→ With a mortar and pestle, combine and grind to a powder the anise seed, juniper berries, salt, and pepper. Set aside.

→ Wipe the moisture from the duck breast with paper towels. Lay the duck down, fat facing up. Using a sharp paring knife, score the fat in a crisscross pattern. You want to go down deep enough in the fat without piercing the flesh. Take your time with this. The deeper into the fat you go, the more it will crisp up.

→ Rub the spice mix all over the duck, including over the fat.

→ In a saucepan, add the balsamic vinegar and Madeira wine. Cook on medium heat until the liquid has reduced by half. Add the chicken stock and again reduce the liquid to half. Add the brown sugar, rosemary, and blueberries. Cook for 5 minutes. The berries will become nice and plump.

→ Remove from heat and strain through a sieve over a saucepan. Press the berries with a wooden spoon to get all the juices into the pan. Return the strained liquid to medium heat, and discard the solids. Add one pat of butter at a time, whisking constantly until all the butter is gone. Leave on the heat, set at simmer.

→ Place a heavy sauté pan on the stovetop. Do not put any cooking oil in the pan. Turn the heat on medium to medium high. Once the pan is hot, lay the duck in the pan, fat side down. In addition, turn on your stove fan. Cook for 10–15 minutes to get it super crispy. You will notice that there will be a large amount of fat in the pan that starts to brown and smoke. Turn the stove off. Using tongs, gently turn the duck so the crispy side is facing up. The hot fat in the pan will continue to cook the duck. Depending on desired doneness, cook for at least 5 minutes for rare. Remove the duck from the pan, and let it cool slightly on a cutting board.

→ Cut the duck meat, and serve with the blueberry sauce and our Wild Rice Cakes (page 30).

All Hail, Sarah Hale

Sarah Josepha Hale (1788–1879)

We have Sarah to thank for today's version of Thanksgiving. Hale wrote to five presidents over a period of seventeen years to petition the feast to be observed as a national holiday. Zachary Taylor, Millard Fillmore, Franklin Pierce, and James Buchanan ignored her requests. It was Abraham Lincoln who finally took the request to heart and acted on it. Persistence eventually paid off. In 1863, it was finally declared a national day of celebration. Before that, there were only two other national holidays on the calendar: George Washington's birthday and Independence Day.

More on Mrs. Hale

Sarah was born in Newport, New Hampshire, and was well-educated as a child. She went on to be the editor of *Godey's Lady's Book* (eventually known as the *Ladies' Magazine*) for over forty years. She had several novels published, and—get this—she wrote a little nursery rhyme you may have heard of, "Mary Had a Little Lamb" (originally titled "Mary's Lamb"). She was extremely outspoken for girls' education reform and advocated for girls and women to enter respectable professions, such as teaching and medicine.

The Mother of Thanksgiving, Sarah Josepha Hale

FUN FACT

Even more impressive—she did not retire until 1877 at the age of eighty-nine. You go, girl.

Mary Ate a Little Lamb

Traditional Scotch broth: a filling soup with lamb and root vegetables.

INGREDIENTS

2 Tbsp olive oil
2 lb lamb shank
1 large onion, quartered
1 cup red wine (we used Cabernet Sauvignon)
8 cups boiling water
3 tsp salt, divided
2 tsp pepper, divided
2 bay leaves
2 Tbsp butter
2 leeks (white portion), cleaned and trimmed
3 carrots, peeled and thinly sliced
1 celery, finely diced
1 turnip, cut in small cubes
2 cloves garlic, minced
2 lb lamb stew meat
3 Tbsp all-purpose flour
1 tsp ground coriander
2 sprigs thyme
1 cup pearl barley

DIRECTIONS

⇥ Make your own lamb stock first. In a large stockpot, heat olive oil on medium-high heat. Add the shanks and onions, browning the meat. Once brown, remove the shanks and onions, and add the wine. Scrape up any of the brown bits. Add the shanks and onions back to the pan, and cook for 20 minutes.

⇥ To the pot, add the boiling water, 1½ tsp salt, 1 tsp pepper, and bay leaves. Raise the heat until the liquid begins to boil. Drop the temperature to simmer, partially cover, and cook for 2 hours.

⇥ Remove the shanks and onions from the pot and set aside for later. Discard the bay leaves and strain the stock. Cool in the refrigerator.

⇥ On medium-high heat, melt butter in the stockpot. Add the leeks, carrots, celery, turnip, and garlic. Cut the onions that have been set aside, which you previously used in the stock, and add back to the pot. Cook until the vegetables become soft.

⇥ While the vegetables are cooking, combine the lamb stew meat in a plastic bag with flour, coriander, and the remaining 1½ tsp salt and 1 tsp pepper. Place your hands on the outside of the bag and mix, ensuring that each piece of meat is covered with the seasonings.

⇥ Lower the heat to medium. Add the lamb stew meat and any leftover flour from the plastic bag, the lamb shanks, thyme, barley, and the lamb stock, about 8 cups. If you have less stock than required, add either beef stock or water until you have 8 cups. Raise the heat again to boil, then drop the heat back down to simmer for 2 hours.

⇥ If you like the flavor of lamb shank, you can shred the meat into the finished soup, or you can discard.

Boston Light was the first lighthouse to be built in the New World. It was first manned by Mr. George Worthylake in 1718. The tower was destroyed by British troops in 1776, but it was lovingly rebuilt in 1783.

1650s to 1680s: Time to Thrive

Grow and Prosper

We do not want to just survive; we want to live and thrive!

A few decades after the first landing, when everyone was settling into their new land and finding their way around the challenges of surviving, the colonies began to grow and prosper. Imports were coming in and exports were going out. This meant better cooking tools, ingredients, and methods. Our melting pot of a country began to utilize lessons taught from settlers who came from all over the world.

We actually ate *better* than most Europeans. Throughout the United Kingdom, eating a combination of meat and wheat flour was a sign of wealth, whereas the colonists were having meat every day. Widespread famine was not a problem here as it was in countries such as Ireland and England. Those in the Northeast regularly ate beef, pork, veal, and lamb; they also kept chickens, turkeys, geese, and ducks.

Imports such as fortified wines, rum, raisins, currants, lemons, and nutmeg all made their way to the ports along the East Coast, making meals that much more enjoyable. Creativity was key as they used imports and native ingredients to create what we now consider classic all-American dishes.

Also during this time, the fishing industry began to take off. Although the Native Americans had first taught the settlers how to fish, the settlers turned their newfound skills into a thriving business. Cod was the colonists' cash cow. Cha-ching. It was widely sought after throughout the world, and the fish were dried, salted, and sold to Europeans.

Cheap Sweets

Molasses was an interesting ingredient—it was not popular with the Europeans so much, but it quickly became a staple in the colonial home. Settlers in the Northeast used it with baked beans, soups, and marinades, and they even mixed it with bourbon. It was used in baking desserts and breads and used as a treat for kids when mixed with milk. Unfortunately, its checkered past involves what was called the Triangular Trade—a lousy triangle of trade between Africa, the Caribbean, and New England, which moved molasses, rum, and slaves among the three locations. While molasses was considerably cheaper than sugar, it came at an ultimate price that left a dark mark on American history.

Other exports by region include:

New England	Middle Colonies	Southern Colonies
Cattle	Horses	Tobacco
Lumber	Beer	Fruit
Fish	Flax	Lumber
Fur	Apples	Clay
Corn	Rope	Beaver
Whale products	Bricks	Iron
Raw wool	Tobacco	Rice
Dried meats	Bread	Silkworms
Wheat flour		Furniture
		Olives
		Capers
		Pottery
		Pork

Veal with Madeira Sauce

We based this on the old recipe for Scotch collops.

INGREDIENTS

¾ lb veal cutlet
1 cup all-purpose flour
½ tsp nutmeg, plus 1/8 tsp for the sauce
¼ tsp salt, plus extra to taste
¼ tsp pepper, plus extra to taste
1 large egg, beaten
At least 1 Tbsp unsalted butter
1 small onion, thinly sliced (we used a sweet
   onion)
1 large clove garlic, minced
½ cup Madeira wine
½ cup chicken stock
1/8 tsp cinnamon
1 Tbsp mascarpone
Flat leaf parsley, minced (optional)

DIRECTIONS

→ Place veal cutlets between two pieces of wax paper, and lightly pound until ¼-inch thick.

→ Mix flour, ½ tsp nutmeg, ¼ tsp salt, and ¼ tsp pepper in a shallow dish. In a separate shallow dish, add the egg.

→ Pat veal dry with paper towels. Dunk veal into the egg, followed by the flour mixture, and set aside. Repeat until all pieces are covered.

→ In a deep sauté pan, add 1 Tbsp butter and melt on medium heat. Cook veal, 2 minutes each side (we are serious about the cooking time!). Add additional pats of butter as needed; you do not want the veal to burn. Veal is light, delicate meat—overcooking happens in seconds, and it can ruin your entire dish. If your veal is thicker or thinner than recommended, adjust your cooking time. Place cooked veal on a plate and set aside.

→ In the same sauté pan, add onions and garlic. Cook until the onions start to become tender. Add Madeira, scrape up all the cooking bits at the bottom of the pan, and stir. Add chicken stock, cinnamon, and 1/8 tsp nutmeg. Once all the ingredients fully incorporate into the sauce, add the mascarpone, and salt and pepper to taste. Return the veal to the pan, spooning the sauce and onions over the veal.

→ Serve immediately over our Creamy Parsnip and Turnip Mash (page 42). If you want to be fancy, sprinkle a dash of minced flat leaf parsley.

Blueberry Layer Cake

During the first Forefathers' Day on December 22, 1769, the members of the Old Colony Club served a large baked Indian whortleberry pudding. Whortleberries are European blueberries that grow on shrubs, similar to huckleberries. Since most grocery stores today do not stock whortleberries or huckleberries, we created this dish with blueberries. This moist four-layer cake is not too sweet, which allows the star of the cake, blueberries, to shine.

INGREDIENTS

Buttermilk Batter:
1 cup all-purpose flour, plus extra to prepare pan
1 stick unsalted butter, room temperature, plus extra to prepare pan
¼ tsp baking soda
¼ tsp salt
⅛ tsp baking powder
½ cup buttermilk
⅔ cup sugar
1 large egg white
½ tsp vanilla paste

Crumble Layer:
1½ cups all-purpose flour
½ tsp cinnamon
3 Tbsp old-fashioned oats
¾ cup brown sugar, packed
⅓ cup sugar
½ tsp vanilla paste
1 stick butter, unsalted, melted

Final Preparation:
4–4½ cups blueberries, rinsed and dried, divided

DIRECTIONS

Buttermilk Batter

* Heat oven to 350 degrees. Butter and flour the cake pan with extra butter and flour.

* In a mixing bowl, combine flour, baking soda, salt, and baking powder. Set aside. Pour the buttermilk in a small bowl and set aside.

* In a stand mixer, cream butter. Add sugar, and mix until fully incorporated. Add egg white, followed by the vanilla paste. Shut mixer off, and scrape the sides down with a spoon. Turn mixer back on to low.

* Alternate adding in the buttermilk and flour mixture in the mixer. Between each set, scrape down the sides of the bowl. We blended in three sets. This mixture is going to be thick and sticky.

Crumble Layer

* Using a food processor, blend the flour, cinnamon, oats, brown sugar, sugar, and vanilla paste. Do not over-blend; spend just enough time to mix the oats into the flour. While the processor is on, pour the melted butter into the mixture. Remove the bowl from the processor, and manually stir the mixture to ensure that the butter is incorporated.

Final Preparation

- In the prepared pan, add 2–2½ cups blueberries to the bottom of the pan in a single layer.

- Using a plastic spatula, add spoonfuls of the buttermilk batter to the top of the blueberries. Go slowly, and be patient. Once all of the buttermilk batter is on top of the blueberries, slowly spread the batter to form a single layer; we used a frosting knife.

- Layer the batter with the remaining blueberries, again in a single layer. Finish the cake by spreading the crumble layer over the top, pressing down lightly. If you have extra crumble topping and blueberries, add them to a ramekin and make a quick blueberry crumble. Bake the cake for 50 minutes.

- This is best enjoyed when cooled or even chilled in the refrigerator.

Creamy Parsnip and Turnip Mash

Root veggie heaven! Yes, we used mascarpone . . . do not judge.

INGREDIENTS

1–1½ cups potato, peeled and diced (we used russet)
5 cups turnips, peeled and diced (we used purple top turnips)
2 cups parsnips, peeled and diced
Generous pinch salt, plus extra to taste
8 Tbsp unsalted butter
1½ Tbsp fresh sage, minced
½ cup heavy cream
½ cup mascarpone
Pepper, to taste

DIRECTIONS

⇒ Place potato, turnips, and parsnips in a deep pan. Cover with water, a generous pinch of salt, and stir. Cook vegetables until they are tender.

⇒ While vegetables are cooking, add butter and sage in a saucepan. Once butter is completely melted, slowly drizzle in the heavy cream. Simmer until the vegetables in the other pan are ready. Do not let the cream boil or bubble over. The idea here is to ensure that the milk is incorporated into the butter, and the cream is warm.

⇒ Drain vegetables and place them in a mixing bowl on a stand mixer. Turn mixer on. As vegetables are being mashed, slowly pour in the warm milk mixture. Mix until it reaches a desired consistency. Do not stir too long as they will get gummy.

⇒ Add the mascarpone, and stir. Salt and pepper to taste.

⇒ Suggestion: Serve with Veal with Madeira Sauce (page 39).

Baked Stuffed Lobster Tails

The classic New England seafood dish that celebrates the bounty from local fisherman. Today, you can live anywhere in the world and still have access to fresh seafood from New England to make your own baked stuffed lobster tails.

INGREDIENTS

6 raw lobster tails*
2 cups Ritz crackers, crushed into crumbs
1 cup panko
4 cloves garlic, minced
1/3 cup parsley, chopped
8 Tbsp butter, unsalted, melted, divided
4 large raw shrimp, cleaned, deveined, and
    minced
1/4 lb raw scallops, cleaned, trimmed, and minced
1 Tbsp Worcestershire sauce
2 Tbsp lemon juice
1 tsp salt
1/2 tsp white pepper

DIRECTIONS

⇥ Set oven to 400 degrees. Prepare the lobster tails by cutting the flesh down the middle of the tail with a paring knife. This will make room for all that yummy stuffing.

⇥ Combine the crackers, panko, garlic, parsley and 6 Tbsp butter. In the same bowl, add the shrimp, scallops, Worcestershire sauce, lemon juice, salt, and pepper, and mix well together. The mixture should be moist from the liquids, but not wet. Spoon the stuffing into the lobster, pressing down with your hands.

⇥ Pour the remaining melted 2 Tbsp butter over the top (because everything tastes better with butter) and cook for 15–20 minutes or until golden on top.

*TIP

You can purchase lobster tails at your local grocery store. If you are lucky enough to have a reputable fish market near you, they can prepare the tails using live lobsters. Just take the rest of the meat for noshing later.

Corn from the Ashes

And by "ashes," we mean "bacon"! A fantastic side dish for . . . well . . . anything.

INGREDIENTS

1 lb bacon, cut into bite-sized pieces
5 fresh sage leaves, roughly chopped
1 tsp cinnamon
1 tsp ground ginger
½ tsp chili pepper
1 stick unsalted butter, melted
4 ears corn

DIRECTIONS

- On medium-high heat, cook the bacon in a covered Dutch oven until it starts to crisp. Uncover, stir, and cook until bacon is crisp, not burnt. Shut heat off and allow the bacon to render and cool slightly. Once cooled, using a slotted spoon, remove the bacon and place on a plate lined with paper towels. Set aside. Pour the bacon fat into a sealed container to use later for cooking all kinds of great stuff.

- Turn oven on to 350 degrees. If you have a roasting feature on your stove like we do, that is a better option.

- In a blender, combine the cooked bacon, sage, cinnamon, ground ginger, and chili pepper. Give it a couple of pulses to mix the items. While the blender is on, pour the butter into the bacon mix, and blend until incorporated and chopped.

- Prepare corn by placing them on 4 pieces of aluminum foil. Spoon the bacon mixture evenly over the corn. Using your hands, smear the bacon mixture over the entire piece of corn.

- Seal the aluminum foil around the bacon-smeared corn. Place the sealed corn in a deep baking pan to prevent the butter from leaking, and roast for 45 minutes.

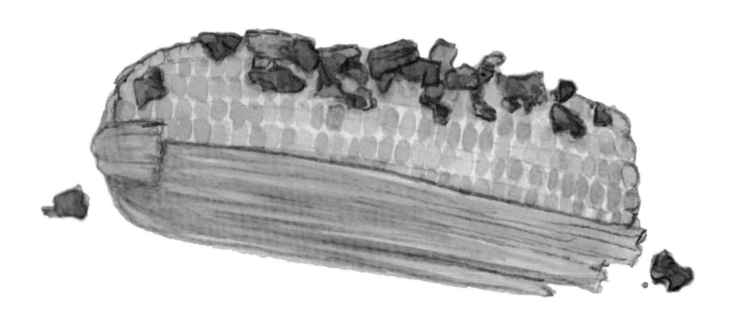

Late 1600s: Bake Away and Satisfy Your Sweet Tooth

Baking Rises to a New Level

Let them eat cake!

As ships made their way into various ports along the East Coast of the New World, supplies, tools, and skilled artisans came to shore. While the colonists continued to utilize their new skills and native ingredients, they now had access to sugar, baking dishes, wafer irons, and butter churns (once considered a luxury).

Baking bread went from being a *very* labor-intensive process to a less time-consuming chore. The colonists' creativity in mixing the old with the new led to some interesting results. For example, colonists in the South used ground rice and dried pumpkin to make biscuits and potatoes for muffins. Other breadstuff included:

Johnnycakes or journey cakes: cornmeal, boiling water, and salt

Ashcakes: cornmeal, grease, and water baked in cabbage leaves and cooked in the smoldering ashes of a fire

Scratch-backs: hardened corn pudding with a rough, uneven surface

Seedcakes: made with caraway seeds

As sugar and syrups arrived on the docks, desserts finally began to be more than just preserved fruit. Creative cooks produced sweet concoctions that quickly became popular in the taverns and wealthier homes:

Flummery: a cream custard thickened by the gelatin of a calf's foot and topped with nuts and fruit

Syllabub: cream curdled with lemon, wine, sugar, and a whipped froth topping

Whitspots: bread pudding in pastry

Also popular were cobblers, fruit pies, spice cakes, pound cake, gingerbread, trifles, and beggar's pudding, which consisted of cut-up stale bread (resourceful!) mixed with nuts, spices, and wine. There was candy too—rock candy, candied lemon peels, and maple-flavored treats.

Sally Lunn Muffins

There is a lot of confusion as to whether or not Sally Lunn was a real woman. Some say she was a French pastry chef living in England, others say it is simply a reference to the sun and moon—soleil et lune in French—because of the bun's coloring: light on top, dark on the bottom. Whatever the real story is, this delicious breakfast bread was said to be George Washington's favorite.

INGREDIENTS

2 cups whole milk
2 Tbsp unsalted butter, melted (plus extra for greasing)
1 cup brown sugar, packed
2 eggs, beaten
4½ tsp yeast (or 2 packets)
5½ cups bread flour
½ tsp salt
1 tsp ground cardamom

DIRECTIONS

⇥ In a saucepan, heat the milk and butter. Do not boil or scald; just warm enough for the butter to melt. Remove from heat once the butter and milk are fully incorporated.

⇥ In a standing mixer, add the brown sugar. While the paddle is going, slowly pour in the warm milk mixture. Allow the sugar to dissolve and blend with the milk. Stop mixing and allow the mixture to slightly cool. The ideal feel is warm, not hot.

⇥ Turn the mixer back on at medium speed, and slowly add the eggs. Turn the mixer off, add the yeast, and then turn the mixer back on at the lowest speed for a few rotations of the paddle. This is to mix the yeast into the liquid. Shut the mixer off and allow the yeast to sit for 15 minutes. You will notice the yeast start to bubble.

⇥ While the yeast is processing, sift the flour, salt, and cardamom together. After you have waited for the yeast to bubble, turn the mixer back on to low and add the flour mixture, fully incorporating it. Do not over-stir; it is okay for the dough to look lumpy. Turn off the mixer.

⇥ Remove the dough from the mixer and form into a ball with your hands. Place the dough into a large mixing bowl that has been lightly greased with butter. Dampen a kitchen towel with warm water. Set the towel over the bowl and leave it in on the counter for 2½ hours.

⇥ Set oven to 350 degrees. Grease a deep muffin pan with butter. The dough is going to feel a little like soft taffy. Using a spoon, coax the dough into the pan, filling ¾ of each cup. The dough will rise while baking. Re-cover the remaining dough in the mixing bowl until you are ready to use.

⇥ Cook the dough in the muffin pan for 30 minutes, or until golden. Cool, and pop out of the pan. Continue the steps with the remaining dough until gone. Serve with our Cranberry and Orange Honey Butter (page 50).

Cranberry and Orange Honey Butter

These fall flavors will be a perfect addition to your Thanksgiving meal. The beautifully pink butter spread is so good, you will want to enjoy it anytime of the year. Lovely on warm rolls, toast, or even vegetables like green beans.

INGREDIENTS

1 cup whole cranberries
¼ cup orange juice or water
Zest of 1 orange
Pinch of salt
¼ cup honey
2 sticks unsalted butter, cut into pats

DIRECTIONS

→ In a saucepan, on medium heat, add the cranberries and orange juice (or water). Cook until the cranberries begin to pop open. Strain the cranberries and juice through a sieve. It is best to use a plastic spatula or wooden spoon to push as much juice as possible through the sieve. Put the strained juice back into the pan, discard the solids, and heat the pan on medium once again.

→ Add the orange zest, salt, and honey to the mixture. Stir.

→ Add the pats of butter, a little at a time, stirring until all of the butter has melted. The butter will be a pretty shade of pink.

→ Pour the mixture into jam jars and store in the refrigerator. Serve with our Sally Lunn Muffins (page 49) or give as a gift!

Eggs Benedict-ish on Johnnycakes

Johnnycake or journey cake is typically a cornmeal flatbread. Step aside, English muffins—these are much tastier.

INGREDIENTS

Johnnycake:
1¼ cups buttermilk
1 cup cornmeal
1 Tbsp unsalted butter, plus extra for cooking the Johnnycake
3 Tbsp grated cheese (we used Parmesan)
1 cup self-rising flour
1 tsp salt
1 Tbsp sugar
1 tsp baking powder
2 eggs, whisked

Eggs Benedict-ish:
½ cup grated Parmesan cheese
⅓ cup heavy cream
White vinegar
4 eggs
Smoked salmon
Sautéed asparagus

DIRECTIONS

Johnnycake:

→ On medium-low heat, warm buttermilk, cornmeal, and 1 Tbsp butter in a saucepan. Remove from stove once butter melts and the cornmeal thickens. Add grated cheese.

→ In a large bowl, combine flour, salt, sugar, and baking powder. Slowly pour the buttermilk mix into the dry ingredients, stirring with a wooden spoon constantly. Add the eggs and mix. Allow to rest for 15 minutes, at room temperature.

→ On a griddle or large pan, melt extra butter and place a good dollop of Johnnycake batter on the hot pan. Flip after they rise and are golden. Repeat. Of course, you can eat the Johnnycake the way it is with some Vermont maple syrup— or you can make Eggs Benedict-ish (see below)!

Eggs Benedict-ish

→ In a saucepan, combine Parmesan cheese and heavy cream. Cook on medium to medium-low heat; you do not want to boil this mixture. Ideally, you want to take your time cooking this, allowing it to thicken. Lower the heat to simmer, keeping it warm until you are ready.

→ Time to make the poached eggs. Fill another saucepan with water. Add a capful of white vinegar to the water. Cook on high, and bring it to a rolling boil. While you are waiting for the water to boil, prepare the eggs. We like to crack an egg into a cup or ramekin. Once the boiling water is ready, drop the heat down to low and let the water rest for a minute. Gently slip the egg into the hot water, one at a time. Cook each egg for 4 minutes, to get a nice runny yolk.

→ Lay a Johnnycake on a plate, add some sautéed asparagus and a few slices of salmon, top with the egg, and apply the finishing touch with a nice helping of the cream sauce.

Carrot Pudding

AKA heaven from a Bundt pan.

INGREDIENTS

2 cups carrots, peeled
1 stick unsalted butter, room temperature (plus
   extra for greasing)
1½ cups all-purpose flour
¾ tsp salt
1 tsp baking soda
1 tsp cinnamon
½ tsp nutmeg, and a dash for the glaze
¼ tsp cloves
1 tsp ground ginger
½ cup sugar
½ cup brown sugar, packed
½ cup molasses
5 eggs, large
1 tsp sherry
1 tsp vanilla
1 cup currants
½ cup crème fraiche, room temperature
¼ cup powdered sugar

DIRECTIONS

- Shred the carrots with your food processor, using the shredding blade, and set aside. It is important to prepare the carrots as recommended—thin, matchstick-size carrot pieces will blend beautifully with the ingredients, enhancing the flavor.

- Set oven to 350 degrees. Butter a Bundt or fluted pan. In a large bowl, combine flour, salt, baking soda, cinnamon, nutmeg, cloves, and ginger. Set aside.

- In a standing/hand mixer, whip 1 stick butter and then add the white sugar, followed by the brown sugar. Add the molasses and mix well. Next, add the eggs, one at a time, while beating. Once the mixture is well-blended, lower the speed of the mixer and add the sherry, vanilla, and currants.

- Next, slowly add the dry flour mixture while beating. Finish the batter by adding in the carrots. Beat a few times at a slow speed and then turn it off.

- Add the mixture to the buttered pan, and tightly cover the pan with aluminum foil. This is an important process because the batter is cooked in two different ways—by the heat of the oven and by the steam within the pan. It makes for a moist cake! Cook for 55 minutes.

- While the cake is cooking, make the glaze. Combine the crème fraiche, powdered sugar, and a dash of nutmeg.

- When the cake is done, remove from the oven. Allow to slightly cool, and then invert the pan onto a plate. Smother the top with the crème fraiche glaze. If you find that the cake is not inverting, a butter knife around the side helps, as well as tapping the pan on the counter. If that does not work, cut a slice, add the glaze, and enjoy—it is delicious either way.

chicken Dumplings

What came first, the chicken or the dumplings?

INGREDIENTS

Dumplings:
1 cup buttermilk
1 egg, beaten
2 Tbsp fresh chives, chopped
1 tsp salt
1 tsp pepper
2 cups rotisserie chicken meat, shredded
1½ cups self-rising flour
2 tsp baking powder

Sauce:
3 Tbsp unsalted butter
2 cloves garlic, minced
1 large onion, chopped
2 large carrots, thinly sliced
1 large stock celery, thinly sliced
½ tsp salt
¼ cup flour, all-purpose
6 cups chicken stock
4 sprigs fresh thyme
½ tsp pepper
½ cup peas (we used baby sweet peas)
½ cup flat leaf parsley, chopped

DIRECTIONS

Dumplings:

↯ In a large mixing bowl, add the buttermilk, egg, chives, salt, and pepper, and whisk. Add the chicken meat and stir until fully mixed. Lastly, add the flour and baking powder and mix with a large wooden spoon. Once you can tell that the flour is fully incorporated, stop mixing. Over-mixing the flour can create a dense dumpling. Set the bowl aside.

Sauce:

↯ Over medium heat, add butter to a Dutch oven. Add the garlic, onions, carrots, celery, and salt to the pot, and cook for about 5–7 minutes until the vegetables become tender. Add the flour to the vegetables and stir for 3 minutes.

↯ Slowly pour in 1 cup chicken stock and stir until the flour dissolves. Add the remaining stock, stir, and follow it with sprigs of thyme, pepper, and peas. Raise the heat to medium-high and boil.

↯ Drop spoonfulls of dumpling batter into the thick broth. The dumplings are going to double in size when cooking, so be careful not to crowd the soup.

↯ Lower the heat to simmer, and cover the pot for 20 minutes. Do not open the cover, as you need the steam to cook the dumplings. After 20 minutes, uncover the pot and test the dumplings with a toothpick to ensure that they are done.

↯ Sprinkle with parsley, and serve.

Shoofly Pie Ice Cream

Shoofly pie was developed in Pennsylvania as a traditional Dutch dish that was always made with molasses. They liked to eat this pie with coffee for breakfast. We have taken the essence of the original dish and turned it into ice cream! *

INGREDIENTS

2 cups whole milk
1¼ cups heavy cream
¾ cup brown sugar
¼ cup molasses
¼ tsp vanilla
¼ tsp cinnamon
½ tsp ground nutmeg
6 large egg yolks

Crumble Topping (Optional):

1½ cups flour
¾ cup sugar
1 tsp cinnamon
½ tsp nutmeg
⅛ tsp salt
1 stick unsalted butter, melted

*TIP
You will need an ice-cream maker for this recipe.

DIRECTIONS

- In a saucepan over medium heat, combine milk, cream, brown sugar, molasses, vanilla, cinnamon, and nutmeg. Bring to a light boil. Adjust heat to low, and simmer.

- Place the egg yolks in a separate bowl. Slowly add 1 tsp of the hot milk mixture to the eggs, stirring constantly until the eggs are tempered. You want them to slowly rise to the same temperature as the mixture to prevent cooking the eggs. Pour the tempered eggs into the saucepan and stir.

- Raise the heat to medium-low; continue to cook and stir until the mixture becomes thick and coats the back of a wooden spoon.

- Strain the mixture and add it to your ice-cream maker. Make ice cream as directed by your ice-cream maker. We popped ours into the freezer for firmness.

Crumble Topping (Optional):

- If you are one of the folks who love the crumble topping of a shoofly pie, we further suggest making this quick, optional topping: Preheat the oven to 350 degrees. Combine flour, sugar, cinnamon, nutmeg, salt, and butter. Add the mixture to a shallow baking pan, and toast in the oven until golden. Set aside to cool, then sprinkle over the top of a heaping bowl of shoofly pie ice cream.

Apple Pie Tiramisu

The added benefit of this dessert is learning how to make your own vanilla pudding—it is incredibly easy, quick, and delicious . . . and you know what is in each bite.

INGREDIENTS

Vanilla Pudding:
2 cups whole milk
½ cup heavy cream
½ cup sugar
1 Tbsp vanilla paste
1 large whole egg and 2 large egg yolks
3½ Tbsp cornstarch
¼ tsp salt
3 Tbsp unsalted butter

Tiramisu:
1½ cups whipping cream
1 Tbsp confectioners' sugar
¼ tsp nutmeg
¼ tsp ground cloves
3 tsp cinnamon, divided
1 stick unsalted butter
5 apples, peeled and diced (we used Granny Smith)
¾ cup sugar

¼ tsp salt
5 Tbsp apple brandy or Laird's Applejack*
5 Tbsp apple cider
1 package crispy ladyfingers

DIRECTIONS

Vanilla Pudding:

 In a saucepan, cook the milk and cream on medium heat. Slowly bring it to a simmer, while stirring frequently. The bubbles on the surface are your sign to remove it from the heat; do not let the milk boil.

 In a mixing bowl, combine the sugar, vanilla paste, whole egg and yolks, cornstarch, and salt with a whisk. You want the texture to become creamy and somewhat airy. Using a tablespoon, start to slowly stream the hot milk into the egg mixture—this technique is called tempering. You want to raise the egg temperature slowly so that the mixtures can be combined without scrambling the eggs. Once the egg mixture is at a warm temperature, pour it into the saucepan. Add the butter, and cook the combined mixture over medium heat for about 10 minutes, or until the pudding becomes thick.

 Pour the pudding through a sieve into a bowl (this will make sure any cooked eggs will be captured and discarded).

 Cover the surface of the pudding with plastic wrap and chill in the refrigerator for about 1 hour or more.

> ## *TIP
> If you want a more intense flavor, increase the amount of alcohol and decrease the apple cider.

Tiramisu:

↠ In a stand mixer, combine the whipping cream, confectioners' sugar, nutmeg, cloves, and 1 tsp cinnamon. Beat with a whisk blade until light and airy. Gently, fold the whipped cream into the vanilla pudding. Here is a helpful option: Pour the pudding into a large plastic bag followed by the whipped cream and lightly combine the two mixtures using your hand. Chill the bag in the refrigerator until you are ready. By cutting a small hole in the corner of the bag, you now have an easy piping bag to apply this mixture to your tiramisu.

↠ In a sauté pan, melt the butter and add the apples, sugar, remaining cinnamon, and salt. Cook until the apples are tender and the other ingredients have created a syrup. Remove from the heat, and set aside in a bowl.

↠ Time to pull it all together. In a pie plate or a shallow bowl, add the liquor and cider, and give each ladyfinger a quick dunk. Caution: do not leave the ladyfingers in the bowl as they will turn to mush.

↠ We used an 8-inch springform pan for functionality as well as appearance. Create layers in the springform pan, starting with the cream, then the ladyfingers, followed by the apple mixture. Repeat all the steps one more time, with a final and third layer of cream on the top. You may need to break a ladyfinger or two to make it fit around the pan—don't worry, it will taste great. Perhaps sprinkle some of your favorite warm spices on the top.

↠ Cover with plastic wrap and chill for at least 3 hours. However, we do recommend chilling overnight.

Salem's Plot

It is no secret that the theories behind the cause of the Salem witch hunts of 1692 range from absolutely absurd to somewhat reasonable. One theory involves rye and its effects on the human body.

The area of Danvers and Salem was overcrowded and fraught with crop failures, drought, disease, land disputes, religious turmoil, and death. Many of the new inhabitants were fleeing from the North due to the destruction from King Philip's War on the colonists. These factors certainly contributed to the paranoia and suspicion that took over the town. Someone *had* to be responsible for the series of unfortunate events, and that someone was the devil himself, according to Reverend Samuel Parris, a Puritan minister who first made the accusations.

Parris's daughter and niece began to exhibit strange behaviors such as mental fits, foreign speech, and convulsions, and the symptoms seemed to spread throughout the village. Soon it was declared as witchcraft. The witch hunt was not limited to Salem; it spread across New England, with a less notorious set of trials in Gloucester, Massachusetts.

Historians have speculated that the strange behaviors could have been explained as schizophrenia, seizure disorders, or encephalitis, but another theory has emerged from the Rensselaer Polytechnic Institute in New York. They claim it was a fungus called ergot found in various grains, especially rye. Rye was a staple for most residents at the time, so this could have very well been the case.

How does ergot affect humans? Hallucinations, irrational behavior, convulsions, confusion, nausea, seizures, vomiting, and sometimes death. Hmm. We wonder if it could cause you to fly on a broom, too. Suspicious, but not conclusive.

Catch Her in the Rye

Mushroom canapés on rye, forego the ergot.

INGREDIENTS

Olive oil
8 slices light rye bread, crust removed
4 Tbsp unsalted butter, divided
3 cloves garlic, minced
1 leek (white part only), trimmed, cleaned, and thinly sliced
8 oz oyster mushrooms, cleaned, trimmed, and diced
7 oz shiitake mushrooms, cleaned, trimmed, and diced
¼ cup chicken stock
½ tsp salt, plus extra to taste (we used black truffle sea salt, which adds great flavor)
¼ tsp pepper, plus extra to taste
½ tsp ground coriander, divided
1 tsp fresh thyme, removed from stems
1 tsp fresh rosemary, removed from stems and minced
½ cup sherry, plus 3 extra Tbsp
3 Tbsp all-purpose flour
4 oz goat cheese
2 tsp honey
Chopped parsley (optional)

DIRECTIONS

→ Set the oven to 375 degrees. Brush the rye bread with olive oil, and cook on that side until golden. Flip the bread over, brush with olive oil, and cook the other side until brown. Turn off the oven, remove toast, and set aside.

→ Heat 2 Tbsp butter in a sauté pan on medium heat. Add the garlic and leek, cooking until soft. Follow with the mushrooms, chicken stock, salt, pepper, and ¼ tsp coriander. Cook until the liquid has evaporated.

→ Sprinkle the mushroom mix with thyme and rosemary, stir, and immediately follow with the sherry.

→ While the flavors are melding, melt the remaining 2 Tbsp butter in a small bowl. Add the flour to the butter, stirring until it forms a paste. Add the flour and butter mix to the sauté pan with the mushrooms. Stir until thick, about 2 minutes. Remove from the heat, and add salt and pepper to taste.

→ In a small pan, warm the goat cheese on medium-low heat. Add the remaining coriander and honey. Once the cheese becomes warm, lower the heat to low.

→ Lay the golden toast on a platter. Add the mushroom ragout, followed by the goat cheese, and sprinkle with parsley if you choose.

The Virginia Ham

Almost everyone has had the pleasure of eating a delicious Virginia ham for Easter or Christmas. The process of curing meats was critical in colonial times. A lack of refrigeration made for some challenging preservation techniques.

To cure meat properly, climate is key. It cannot be too cold or the meat will freeze; it cannot be too hot or it will rot. And the Virginia climate has proven to be ideal. The pigs lucky (or unlucky) enough to be raised in Virginia are fed acorns, nuts, and peaches. When ham is smoked, the process is done over hickory wood fires.

Virginia country hams first began with the Jamestown settlers. Hogs shipped over were kept on an island in the James River, which was known as Hog Island in Surry County. The water served as a barrier to prevent them from escaping. The natives had long been curing venison, but the taste of a cured ham from this area became so popular that it was often shipped over to England for trade. As a result, this was one of the first exports from America.

Most of the companies still producing Virginia hams utilize some of the original methods introduced by the settlers: hickory smoke aged four months. The ham is mildly salty with a touch of sweetness.

Hogs are slaughtered during the winter, the meat is rubbed with salt, and the cool air keeps it from spoiling. Then they are rinsed and hung to dry and smoke in the warmer months.

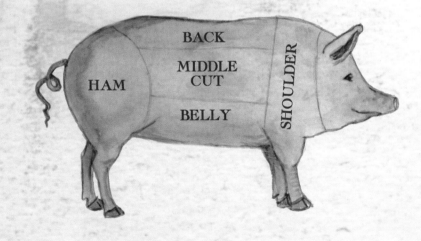

Baked Virginia Ham with Bourbon Orange Glaze

Live high on the hog.

INGREDIENTS

6–8 lb fully cooked ham, bone-in
½ cup bourbon (we used Jim Beam Black)
Juice of 1 orange, about 7 Tbsp (we used a Cara cara orange)
Zest of 1 orange
½ cup brown sugar, packed
½ cup prepared Dijon mustard
15 whole cloves
¼ cup honey

DIRECTIONS

→ Preheat the oven to 350 degrees.

→ Prepare the ham. You can use a boneless ham if you so choose, but the bone intensifies the flavor and is really the best choice. Trim any unnecessary fat. Next, you are going to score all the fat in a diamond pattern. Using a sharp knife, create lines in one direction, and then repeat this in the opposite direction, creating a diamond pattern. Be careful not to cut into the meat, but you do want to score the fat all the way down to the meat. This allows the fat to render and creates an extra crispy layer. Put the ham in a deep roasting pan, and place it in the oven.

→ On the stovetop, combine all the other ingredients in a saucepan on medium heat. Cook until the brown sugar has melted and the liquid begins to take on the appearance of syrup. Baste the ham every ½ hour or so. As you get closer to the end of cooking, pour the remaining liquid over the ham. Basting the ham with frequency allows the sauce to glisten on the top of the ham.

→ Total cooking time in the oven is about 2½ hours or until the internal temperature reads 145 degrees. Remove the ham from the oven and cool. Slice and enjoy.

Roasted Creamed Corn Hash with Maple Pancetta

The combined flavors hit all the right notes: sweet, creamy, salty, crunchy, and good. This recipe should come with a warning . . . addictive. Make extra.

INGREDIENTS

2 cups corn (if using frozen corn, fully thaw and drain)
2½ tsp fresh tarragon, chopped
½ tsp salt, plus extra to taste
½ tsp pepper, plus extra to taste
4 Tbsp olive oil
8 oz pancetta, cut into bite-size pieces
2 Tbsp maple syrup
2 Tbsp unsalted butter
1 cup onion, diced (we used a sweet onion)
½ cup chicken stock
½ cup heavy cream

DIRECTIONS

→ Heat oven at 400 degrees.

→ Combine corn, tarragon, salt, pepper, and olive oil in a bowl. Mix thoroughly and place on a baking sheet. Roast for 15–20 minutes.

→ While the corn is roasting, cook the pancetta on medium-high heat on the stovetop until it is crispy. Drain all but a small amount of fat from the pan, and lower the heat to medium. Stir in maple syrup and continue to stir until the pancetta is caramelized. Hint: turn on your stove fan. Once finished, remove from heat and set aside in a small bowl. The pancetta is going to harden up a bit, but will soften during the final cooking process.

→ In a sauté pan, on medium heat, melt the butter and add the onions. Cook until tender.

→ Add chicken stock, cook down by half, then add cream and cook for a few minutes until combined. Add the pancetta, stirring to break it up, followed by the corn. Cook until desired consistency, then add salt and pepper to taste.

→ Serve as a side dish or small plate.

The White Horse Tavern

The White Horse Tavern is one of our most favorite spots in New England. We highly recommend visiting in the fall or winter—it's very romantic (order a Dark and Stormy at the bar). The two-story building located on Marlborough Street in Newport, Rhode Island, was originally built in 1652 and opened as a tavern in 1673, making it the oldest tavern in the United States.

There was a broad range of clientele in the early days, including colonists, British soldiers, sailors, and *pirates*. In 1702, it was acquired by the legendary pirate, William Mayes, Jr. Mayes had returned to Newport with some serious bounty and took over. However, since it was an embarrassment to have a crazy pirate running a meeting place for the General Assembly, Criminal Court, and City Council, Mayes's run did not last long.

Eventually the building fell into disrepair but was completely restored in 1957 by the Preservation Society of Newport. Visitors can indulge in fresh seafood from the Narragansett Bay and gaze upon the fabulous historical artifacts within its walls.

Itty Bitty Rhode Island Packs a Punch

Rhode Island was founded by Roger Williams in 1636. But it wasn't exactly for good reason. He was banished from Massachusetts because he was outspoken on his views about separating church and state. He bought the land from the Narragansett Indians, and it turned out to be a wise move as Newport became a major player in trade ports.

Personally, when we think of Rhode Island, we think of Rocky Point Amusement Park and their very memorable clam cakes. Unfortunately, the park, which was built in 1847, closed its doors in 1995. Not exactly colonial history, but we needed to mention it in order to explain our next recipe.

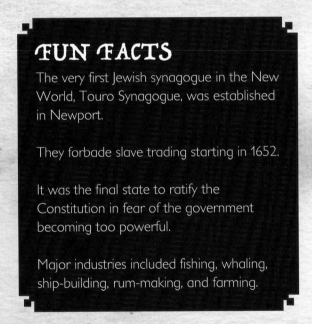

FUN FACTS

The very first Jewish synagogue in the New World, Touro Synagogue, was established in Newport.

They forbade slave trading starting in 1652.

It was the final state to ratify the Constitution in fear of the government becoming too powerful.

Major industries included fishing, whaling, ship-building, rum-making, and farming.

Bacon-Kissed Clam Cakes (Rhody Style)

Please don't call this a fritter to a Rhode Islander.

INGREDIENTS

10 slices bacon
2½ cups self-rising flour
1 Tbsp baking soda
1¼ tsp salt
¼ tsp baking powder
1 Tbsp fresh tarragon, minced
1 tsp garlic powder
2 Tbsp lemon juice
½ cup buttermilk
2 cans (6.5 oz each) minced clams in juice
Cooking oil or lard

DIRECTIONS

➤ Cook the bacon on the stovetop until it is crisp, not burnt. Remove the cooked bacon from the pan and cool on a paper towel. Break the bacon up in small pieces and add to a food processor, along with the flour.

➤ Pulse until the flour starts to change color and the bacon is very small. We must say: bacon flour will become your new best friend after this. The bacon adds smokiness to the flour, which adds a complexity to your recipes. Super easy, with big impact. You're welcome.

➤ In a mixing bowl, combine the bacon flour, baking soda, salt, baking powder, tarragon, and garlic powder. In a small separate bowl, combine the lemon juice, buttermilk, clams, and clam juice. Using a wooden spoon, slowly pour the liquid ingredients into the dry ingredients. Stir while pouring, paying close attention to break down any lumps that have formed. Allow the batter to rest for about 10 minutes at room temperature.

➤ We prefer to use a deep fryer, but you can use a deep fry pan with your choice of cooking oil or lard. Peanut oil is really the most ideal for frying as it has a high smoking point, and it does not leave your food with an odd flavor. Whatever method or oil you choose, make sure you have enough of it. The clam cakes are to be round, or at least roundish. In order to achieve that goal, the batter should be floating in oil. The oil temperature should read between 350 and 360 degrees. Remember, the outside will cook a lot faster than the inside, so make sure that your oil is the right temperature.

➤ Use an ice-cream scooper or a tablespoon to add the batter to the hot oil. Try not to overcrowd the pan. You will hear a nice sizzle when you add the batter to the oil. At first, you may find the batter sticking to the bottom of the pan, but a gentle nudge with a spatula should fix that problem. Brown all sides and cook for about 5 minutes. Place the hot cakes on paper towels to cool; you can also use a clean brown paper bag (soaks up a lot of the oil). Serve as is or with a big bowl of chowder . . . New England style, of course.

The East India Company was an English joint-stock company. Their primary business was to develop trade ventures with the East Indies, and they were relentless in monopolizing all trade routes. After years of government interference and financial disasters, they went out of business in 1874.

1700s to 1790s: Building Our Nation

Let's Have a Tea Party

If you recall your grade school history lessons, you probably think of the Tea Party in these terms: the British taxed the tea, the people revolted, and the next thing you know, crates of tea are floating around Boston Harbor.

Accurate summation, but to elaborate on that: the Boston Tea Party was a midnight raid. On December 16, 1773, a group of colonists disguised themselves as Mohawk Indians, boarded three ships on Griffin's Wharf—the *Dartmouth*, the *Eleanor*, and the *Beaver*—and dumped 342 chests of tea into the water while citizens cheered them on. Ninety thousand pounds of tea were completely undrinkable! The destruction of that much cargo was in protest against the British Parliament's Tea Act of 1773, a bill that essentially gave the East India Company a monopoly on the tea trade. So, the revolt was not due to a major tax hike but rather a protest against a corporate tax break.

The group known as the Sons of Liberty was secretly organized by Samuel Adams (the man, not the beer). Because of the destruction of the tea, Boston Harbor was closed to merchant ships by the British as punishment for their acts, who demanded payment for the destroyed cargo. It was the first major act of rebellion in the colonies, which eventually led to the Revolution and the birth of our nation.

Little known fact: the identities of the men who boarded the ships that night were kept secret, and we still don't know exactly who took part. The Sons of Liberty was a very secret society that recruited members throughout Boston and New York. Meetings were held in taverns owned by those sympathetic to the cause, including the Green Dragon (see page 75).

Another lesser known fact it is that the event was not called the "Boston Tea Party" until the 1820s; it was originally just referred to as the "Destruction of Tea." And what was the cost of this destruction that night? By today's standards, it would've been about one million dollars. Ouch.

Back to a lighter, happier topic—food. By this time, methods of planting, preparation, and preservation had drastically improved. More important, the beer got better. George Washington was a big porter drinker (along with his Madeira; see page 110). His very own recipe for small beer (weak beer) was recorded in 1754 in a private notebook that currently resides in the New York Public Library:

To Make Small Beer:

Take a large Siffer [sifter] full of Bran Hops to your Taste. —Boil these 3 hours then strain out 30 Gall[ons] into a cooler put in 3 Gall[ons] Molasses while the Beer is Scalding hot or rather draw the Melasses [molasses] into the cooler & St[r]ain the Beer on it while boiling Hot. let this stand till it is little more than Blood warm then put in a quart of Yea[s]t if the Weather is very Cold cover it over with a Blank[et] & let it Work in the Cooler 24 hours then put it into the Cask—leave the bung open till it is almost don[e] Working—Bottle it that day Week it was Brewed

We love a man who loves his beer.

Yankee Red Flannel Hash with Braised Cabbage

Ever heard of "bubble and squeak"? We had not either. Bubble and squeak is a dish made from the veggies left over from a roast dinner. Potatoes, cabbage, carrots, peas, etc., are chopped up and fried with mashed potatoes and any leftover meat. It was called by this name because the cabbage made a bubbly or squeaky sound when it was cooked down. Bubble and squeak was served with pickles and sometimes a brown sauce. Here, we've cooked up our own version . . .

INGREDIENTS

Yankee Red Flannel Hash:

1 lb potatoes, peeled and quartered (we used russet as they have high starch levels and crisp up nicely)
2 cups water or vegetable stock
1 Tbsp butter
1 medium onion, sliced thin
2 cloves garlic, minced
8 oz cooked beets, diced*
2 cups red or braised cabbage, cooked and drained (see recipe on page 70)
1 Tbsp fresh chives
2 sprigs fresh thyme, leaves only
1½ tsp sea salt, plus extra to taste
1 tsp white pepper, plus extra to taste
Cooking fat*

*TIP

If you use packaged cooked beets, rinse under water briefly to limit the color bleeding in your food and on anything else the beet juice touches. Use butter or bacon fat for cooking fat—butter will provide richness; bacon fat will add smokiness.

DIRECTIONS

Yankee Red Flannel Hash:

→ Boil potatoes in water or vegetable stock until you can pierce them with a fork. Remove the potatoes from the pan and let cool. Grate potatoes with a manual grater or grater blade on a food processor. Set aside.

→ In a sauté pan, melt butter on medium heat, and add onions. After a few minutes, add the garlic and cook them both tender. Do not brown. Remove from heat.

→ In a large mixing bowl, add the cooked potatoes, onions, and garlic with beets, cabbage, chives, thyme, salt, and pepper to form the hash.

→ Heat a cast-iron pan on medium heat. Cast iron will help you achieve that golden crispy crust; you can also substitute cast iron with a deep fry pan. Add a generous amount of fat to the hot pan. Add enough hash to cover the pan, and press down the hash into the pan. Cook for 5–10 minutes, lifting sides to see if the crust is forming. Once you achieve the desired crust, flip the hash over and repeat on the other side. Salt and pepper to taste.

INGREDIENTS

Braised Cabbage:

1 head red cabbage, cut in half, cored, and sliced
2 Tbsp vegetable oil
1 medium onion, sliced thin
2 Tbsp apple cider vinegar
1 apple, cored, peeled, and diced
1 Tbsp mustard seed
1½ tsp salt
1 Tbsp maple syrup
⅓ cup apple cider
3 sprigs fresh thyme
½ tsp allspice
Salt and pepper, to taste

DIRECTIONS

Braised Cabbage:

→ In a large bowl, soak cut cabbage in water.

→ Heat vegetable oil in a Dutch oven. Add the onion, and cook until tender and translucent. Add the apple cider vinegar to cooked onion and sauté until golden. Add the apple, and stir.

→ Drain cabbage fully, and add to the Dutch oven. Stir in mustard seed, salt, maple syrup, apple cider, thyme, and allspice to the pan. Cover, and cook for 5 minutes on medium-high, while stirring.

→ Cover, reduce heat to medium-low, and cook for 30 minutes or until tender. Salt and pepper to taste.

Braised Short Ribs

Bathed in hard cider, spices, and molasses.

INGREDIENTS

½ cup flour
1½ Tbsp cornstarch
2 tsp salt
2 tsp white pepper
3 lb beef short ribs*
2 Tbsp olive oil, plus extra
1 onion, thinly sliced (about 3 cups)
3 cloves garlic, minced
1 cup carrots, sliced
2 cans (12 oz each) hard cider
1 Tbsp apple cider vinegar
4 Tbsp molasses
2 sprigs thyme, whole
2 tsp allspice
1 tsp nutmeg
¼ tsp cloves
2 tsp ground ginger

DIRECTIONS

➤ In a plastic bag, add flour, cornstarch, salt, and white pepper. Seal the bag and shake to mix. Working in batches, add short ribs to the bag, thoroughly coating each piece. Remove the ribs, shaking off the excess flour, and set aside. Repeat until all the short ribs are coated with flour mixture. Discard remaining flour and bag. Let the short ribs rest at room temperature for 20 minutes.

➤ Heat olive oil in a Dutch oven on medium heat. Working in batches, brown all sides of each short rib. Remove from the pan and set aside.

➤ Add the onion, garlic, and carrots to the pan. Add additional olive oil to prevent the vegetables from burning, but do not overdo it. Cook vegetables until tender.

➤ Add ½ cup hard cider to deglaze the pan. Stir up all the delicious brown bits. Add the rest of the hard cider.

➤ Add apple cider vinegar, molasses, thyme, allspice, nutmeg, cloves, and ground ginger. Since molasses is sticky and difficult to get off the measuring spoons, we swirled the measuring spoons in the cooking liquid to make sure we removed as much molasses as possible.

➤ Add the meat to the cooking liquid. Raise the heat to medium-high until it boils, then lower the heat to medium-low, cover, and cook for 2 hours.

➤ Remove meat and bones from pan. Raise the heat to medium and reduce the liquid by half. While the liquid is cooking down, prepare the short ribs. Short ribs have bones and tough, inedible gristle attached to them. Cut the bone and gristle off the meat, and discard. Once the sauce has thickened, add the meat back to the liquid and cook until the meat is warm again.

➤ Serve the meat with a generous spoonful of sauce. We recommend that you serve this over our Yankee Red Flannel Hash recipe (page 69).

*TIP

Be selective with your purchase. Look for short ribs that are thick and not overly fatty.

Beef Steak Pie

Bake the pies in coffins (narrow pans), and "season the gravy very high," according to Thomas Jefferson. This is the perfect dinner for meat and potato lovers.

INGREDIENTS

1 cup potatoes (we used about 6 mini Yukon
   Gold potatoes)
Chicken stock, enough to cover the potatoes
½ cup flour
2 tsp salt
2 tsp pepper
2 Tbsp cornstarch
1½ lb beef, cut into bite-size pieces (we used
   beef round)
½ cup meat fat, lard, or cooking oil
1 large onion, chopped (about 2 cups)
3 cloves garlic, minced
3 cups boiling water
1 Tbsp Worcestershire sauce
8 Tbsp Madeira wine
5 Tbsp parsley, chopped
Piecrust of your choice
1 sheet puff pastry
1 egg, beaten (optional)

DIRECTIONS

- Cook the potatoes in the chicken stock until the potatoes can just barely be pierced with a fork. Drain, dice, and let cool until ready.

- In a plastic bag, mix the flour, salt, pepper, and cornstarch. Add the beef, seal the bag, and shake. Set aside for 20 minutes or so. Remove the beef from the bag, and shake off any excess flour. Do not discard the flour left in the bag; you will need that shortly.

- Add the meat fat (or any cooking fat or oil) to a Dutch oven on medium heat. Add the beef, working in batches, until browned. Remove meat, and set aside.

- While the Dutch oven is still hot, cook the onions and garlic until soft. Raise the temperature of the heat to medium-high. Add the meat, water, Worcestershire sauce, Madeira, parsley, and whatever flour was left in the plastic bag. Stir until it reaches the boiling point, then drop the heat to simmer and cook for about 1 hour, covered.

- Set oven to 450 degrees and prepare your piecrust. You can use a store-bought crust that comes in its own pan or a favorite homemade piecrust. If you are making your own, we suggest making enough for a deep-dish pan as this is a hearty dish.

- Remove the Dutch oven lid and add the potatoes, gently stirring. Turn the heat off. Now it is time to prepare the pie.

- Using a slotted spoon, add the contents of the Dutch oven onto the piecrust. For effect, make the center a little higher than the sides, making sure you leave enough room for the gravy that is left in the pan. Using a ladle, or a large spoon, pour the gravy over the meat until it gets close to the top.

- Prepare your puff pastry on a flat, well-floured surface. The pastry should be large enough to generously cover the contents in the piecrust. Lay it over the meat pie, seal the edges, and trim the edges where necessary. We recommend brushing the top of the pie with an egg wash (1 egg, beaten).

- Cook for 30 minutes or until nicely golden.

Little Cakes for Tea

Really, they go with anything!

INGREDIENTS

4 sticks unsalted butter, room temperature (plus extra to grease)
4 cups all-purpose flour, plus extra for the pan
1 tsp salt
½ tsp baking powder
¾ cup buttermilk, room temperature
¼ cup orange juice, room temperature (we used about 2 Cara cara oranges)
2 tsp vanilla paste*
3 cups sugar
6 large eggs, room temperature
⅓ cup orange zest (about 6 small oranges)

Optional Glaze:
⅓ cup sugar
⅓ cup Cointreau
⅛ tsp ground cardamom

*TIP
If you cannot find paste, use 2 vanilla beans or vanilla extract.

DIRECTIONS

 Preheat oven to 350 degrees. Prepare a mini muffin pan by greasing it with extra butter, followed by a dusting of flour. Tap the pan upside down to remove any excess flour.

Combine salt, baking powder, and 4 cups flour in a bowl. Set aside. In a separate bowl, combine buttermilk, orange juice, and vanilla. Set aside.

Cream 4 sticks butter and sugar together for about 5 minutes in a stand mixer. Scrape down the sides of the mixing bowl, if necessary. Add the eggs, one at a time, to the mixer, followed by the orange zest. The color of the mixture will become golden.

Alternate adding the dry and wet ingredients into the mixer while the speed is on low.

Add the batter to the muffin pan, and cook until golden. It should spring back a bit when you touch it.

Optional Glaze:

Combine sugar, Cointreau, and cardamom in a small bowl, and stir. Dip the top of the warm cake into the bowl and rest it on a cookie rack. It is best to have a plate underneath to capture any rogue glaze that drips off.

Pumpkin Soup

Stewed pumpkin was a staple for early colonists and Native Americans. We added crisp root vegetables, chicken stock, and honey to elevate this early American favorite.

INGREDIENTS

2 Tbsp unsalted butter
2 large shallots, sliced
1 parsnip, peeled and diced
1 large carrot, peeled and diced
29 oz pumpkin puree
1 quart chicken stock
4 fresh sage leaves, minced
2 tsp salt
1½ tsp white pepper
1 tsp allspice
1 tsp ground ginger
¼ cup honey
½ cup heavy cream

DIRECTIONS

→ In a Dutch oven, melt the butter on medium heat. Sauté the shallots, parsnips, and carrots in the butter until the vegetables soften slightly.

→ Pour the pumpkin puree and chicken stock into the pot with the vegetables, and stir. Sprinkle the sage, salt, pepper, allspice, and ginger into the soup, and stir.

→ Raise the heat to medium-high until it starts to boil. Lower the heat to simmer, add the honey, and cover for 1 hour.

→ Remove the lid and turn off the heat. Using either an emulsion blender or a standard blender, pulse the soup to thicken. (We recommend using the emulsion blender as you have more control; we prefer not to pulverize the parsnip in a standard blender.) This soup has an initial sweetness, but then you will bite into a parsnip for a fresh finish.

→ Pour the cream into the soup, and turn the heat back on to low to warm. As with any soup, this tastes better the next day.

The Green Dragon
"Headquarters of the Revolution"

Although it's not currently located in its original spot, the Green Dragon is worth a visit on your next trip to Boston. This watering hole played a prominent part in America's history. Established in 1654, the Green Dragon got its name from the sign out front—a copper silhouette of a dragon had turned green (patina) from the harsh New England elements. From then on, it was forever known as the Green Dragon.

The original structure was all wood, and it burnt to the ground in the early 1800s. The St. Andrews Lodge of Freemasons bought the building in 1766 and used the basement as a tavern. Secret groups met regularly to discuss the Revolution, including the Sons of Liberty, the Masons, and those planning and plotting the Boston Tea Party. In fact, Paul Revere left from this tavern (after hearing British soldiers discuss their plans to advance) to take his famous ride to Lexington, where he warned John Hancock and Samuel Adams that the British were in fact coming.

Unfortunately, all remaining artifacts burned in the fire. The current location of the Green Dragon is at 11 Marshall Street, right behind the Bell in Hand Tavern. On any given day, you will find a wide range of customers sitting at the bar—people from all over the world as well as those from its own backyard. The regulars (several are history reenactors who give walking tours around Boston) are incredibly friendly and eager to share their stories of people they've met and funny quips about their experiences within the Green Dragon's walls.

On a side note, some historians have disputed the claim that colonists (Revolution activists) could not possibly have overhead British soldiers discussing military tactics at the Green Dragon, that the

British would have never frequented this tavern. Keep in mind, there was not a pub (or Dunkin' Donuts) on every corner in the seventeenth century. It's likely the Green Dragon was the only place to eat and drink within miles. As a result, it's just as likely that the start of Paul Revere's ride was, in fact, spawned by eavesdropping over a pint of ale.

Bell in Hand Tavern

Order the ale. And maybe try the Three Berry Muffin Cocktail.

The Bell in Hand Tavern was established in 1795 by Mr. Jimmy Wilson, the Boston town crier for over fifty years who reported everything from the Boston Tea Party to the birth of our nation. After years of loyal service, Mr. Wilson retired and established the Bell in Hand, its name being a tribute to his former profession.

The Bell in Hand Tavern has moved around a bit since it was founded, but its current address has been in place since 1844, and the building still has original brickwork and granite (and is surrounded by fabulous cobblestone roads.)

Mr. Wilson was well known for his extremely thick ale, so much so that he served it in not one, but two, mugs—one for the delicious ale and a second for the fantastic froth. He was so confident about this ale that he refused to serve the more popular drinks of the time: whiskey, rum, or gin. Nope, just ale.

The current owners of the tavern, Debbie and Adam Kessler, are wonderful and gracious people who are more than happy to discuss the history of the Bell in Hand—and the clam chowder. We begged for the recipe, but it was a firm *no*. So, don't miss ordering the chowder or hot lobster roll if you happen to stop by. And definitely order Mr. Wilson's Bell in Hand Ale.

Boston Brown Bread and Baked Beans

In the past, Boston brown bread was made in a can, oftentimes an old coffee can. We did not use the traditional coffee can to cook the mixture; instead, we used a 1-quart pudding pot. You can find these on Amazon, and they are quite handy to have. Since purchasing a proper pudding pot, I have made brunch items (Plough Pudding from our first book, A Thyme and Place*), cakes, and now the classic Boston brown bread.*

INGREDIENTS

Boston Brown Bread:

1 tsp baking soda
½ tsp salt
¾ cup wheat flour
¾ cup rye flour
½ tsp mace (or nutmeg)
½ cup currants
1 cup buttermilk
⅓ cup molasses
Butter, to prepare the pudding pot

DIRECTIONS

Boston Brown Bread:

- Set oven to 325 degrees. In a large bowl, combine baking soda, salt, the flours, and mace.

- Add the currants to the mix and stir, followed by the buttermilk and molasses. Do not over-mix, but make sure that everything is fully incorporated.

- Use a 1-quart pudding pot or a similar vessel to cook the bread. Butter the inside thoroughly. Boil a large pot of water. The pot should be big enough to hold your cooking vessel and allow the water to go up the side of vessel. Once the water hits the boiling point, turn the heat off.

- Pour the brown bread mixture into the vessel—it should come up about ¾ of the way to the top—leaving extra room for it to rise while cooking. Cover with aluminum foil and tie it tight with twine. Place the vessel in the pot of water, making sure that the hot water does not get into the foil or over the top of the vessel.

- Cook for 1 hour. After 30 minutes of cooking, make sure the water level is around the same height. If it has reduced, add more boiling water to the pan.

- Remove the pans from the oven, and take out the vessel holding the brown bread from the water. Let the vessel cool slightly, about 10 minutes, before you unwrap the foil. Serve the bread warm with a hunk of butter.

INGREDIENTS

Baked Beans:

3 Tbsp salt, divided
1 tsp baking powder
1 lb dried navy beans, rinsed (remove any dark beans)
6 whole cloves
12 oz salt pork, rinsed and cut into small pieces
4 cloves garlic, minced
2-inch piece fresh ginger, minced
1 Tbsp prepared Dijon mustard
½ cup molasses
½ cup brown sugar, packed
1 Tbsp pepper
¼ cup bourbon
¼ cup honey

DIRECTIONS

Baked Beans:

→ In a large container, add 2 quarts of water, 1½ Tbsp salt, and baking powder. Stir. Add the beans in the salty water for at least 8 hours, preferably overnight. After the beans have been soaked, drain the water and rinse the beans well.

→ Cooking baked beans is an example of cooking low (heat) and slow (time). Set the oven temperature to 300 degrees and move the oven rack down a notch to the lower position.

→ Place your Dutch oven on the stovetop and set the heat to medium-high. Combine the beans, cloves, salt pork, garlic, ginger, mustard, molasses, brown sugar, pepper, remaining 1½ Tbsp salt, bourbon, and honey. Stir, and then add enough water to cover the beans by ½ inch. Once the liquid reaches the boiling point, turn the heat on the stovetop off, cover the pot, and place it in the oven.

→ After the beans have been cooking for 1 hour, check to see if there is enough liquid in the pot. The beans should have enough liquid to cover them, so add more water if too much liquid has evaporated. Cook for another hour.

→ Uncover, and continue to cook for an additional hour until the beans are soft and browned. Total cooking time in the oven is about 3 hours. Remove the Dutch oven and let the beans stand uncovered for 20 minutes. Do not try to eat them right away unless you want to burn off the top layer of your mouth.

The First Saint Patrick's Day

It was on March 17, 1737, that the very first celebration of St. Patrick occurred in the United States. The first parade took place in New York in 1762, and Boston hosted theirs a bit later in 1812. Soon, celebrations, parades, and festivals popped up throughout the rest of the states. These gatherings almost always included a large breakfast and many, many toasts in honor of the patron saint of Ireland.

The Charitable Irish Society of Boston first observed the celebration of the saint to honor their heritage. It was not a religious celebration by any means, and no one was drinking green beer and discussing leprechauns with painted shamrocks on their cheeks. As more and more Irish immigrants came to the colonies, societies developed and annual gatherings took place.

Today, corned beef and cabbage is the main dish on Saint Patrick's Day. As you may have heard, corned beef is not Irish at all. It is the product of a developing Irish-American culture here in the United States and was most likely a bacon substitute for the struggling immigrants. As the holiday became more and more popular, it became a splurge to indulge in corned beef, lamb, and other meats previously unaffordable in their homeland. Throw a potato and a cabbage in there, and you've got a hearty meal to work as a foundation for all that ale.

Shepherd's pie, also associated with this holiday, is often confused with cottage pie. While both originated in the United Kingdom and have been around for hundreds of years, shepherd's pie specifically contains lamb while a cottage pie can contain any meat, most likely beef. Both pies always include potatoes.

Thank you, Arthur

Arthur Guinness began brewing his stout in 1759 in Dublin, Ireland, and was soon selling it by the barrel in 1778. As the business was passed down through the family, techniques and consistency were perfected, shipments were reaching as far as New Zealand, and in 1821 exact instructions for a superior porter were

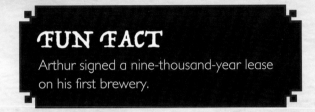

FUN FACT

Arthur signed a nine-thousand-year lease on his first brewery.

recorded, not too far from the Guinness Original and Guinness Extra Stout that we drink today. The first shipment to the colonies was sent in 1817 to South Carolina. It was the death of Prince Albert in 1861 that inspired a London bar to serve a Black Velvet in mourning for the Prince—combining Guinness Extra Stout with Champagne to represent the dark cloud hovering about England.

Saint Arthur's~Sorry, Saint Patrick's~ Guinness and Lamb Shepherd's Pie

INGREDIENTS

2 lb ground lamb meat
2 Tbsp water
2 tsp salt, divided
1 tsp pepper, divided
½ tsp baking soda
7 Tbsp unsalted butter, divided
2 cups onion, chopped (we used sweet onions)
1½ cups oyster mushrooms, trimmed and chopped
1 small turnip, about 1 cup
3 cloves garlic, minced
½ cup Guinness
1 cup beef stock
2 Tbsp flour
2 tsp Worcestershire sauce
3 sprigs thyme, stems removed and discarded
2 bay leaves
2 carrots, peeled and chopped
1 quart chicken stock
2½ lb potatoes, peeled and cut into 1-inch
  pieces (we used a combination of russet and
  white sweet potatoes)
½ cup cream
1 egg yolk, large
2 Tbsp chives

DIRECTIONS

→ Combine lamb meat, water, 1 tsp salt, ½ tsp pepper, and baking soda in a bowl (it is best to use your hands to mix the ingredients). Set aside until ready.

→ In a large cast-iron skillet (we used a 12-inch pan), heat 1 Tbsp butter over medium heat.

Add the onions, mushrooms, remaining 1 tsp salt, remaining ½ tsp pepper, and turnips. Cook until soft and the liquid has evaporated. Add the garlic, stir, and cook for 2 minutes. Add the Guinness, and scrape up any brown bits on the bottom of the pan. Add the beef stock, and heat liquid until it reduces by half.

→ In a small bowl, combine the flour and 2 Tbsp melted butter. Slowly incorporate into the Guinness liquid. Add the Worcestershire, thyme, bay leaves, and carrots. Stir.

→ Reduce the heat to medium-low and add the lamb meat. Use the back of a wooden spoon to break apart the meat. Cover the pan for 10 minutes until the meat is cooked. Remove the cover and the bay leaf. Stir, and drop the heat to low to simmer.

→ Set the oven to 375 degrees. In a stockpot, add the chicken stock and bring to a boil. Add the potatoes and cook until a fork can be easily inserted. Drain thoroughly, and add the potatoes back to the pan.

→ In a small bowl, combine the remaining 4 Tbsp cooled melted butter, cream, egg yolk, and chives. Incorporate the butter mixture with the potatoes using whatever technique you like—we used an emulsion blender. Do not over-mix as the potatoes can get gummy.

→ Add the potatoes to the top of your lamb mixture by piping it out using a plastic bag, with a corner cut out. This technique makes the process easier and presentation nicer, compared to simply plopping the potatoes on top. Use a knife to evenly spread the piped potatoes over the top. Take a fork and draw in wavy lines for presentation.

→ Using both hands (this will be heavy), place the pan on top of a rimmed baking sheet to prevent spillage. Cook in the oven until brown, about 15 minutes.

Franklin Was a Foodie!

Well, if you've ever had to help a child with their history homework (seems this is how we adults get reminded of American History facts), you may have read that Benjamin Franklin was serious about his food. For a short time during his teen years, he was even a vegetarian! He was also big into native ingredients, such as cranberries and maple syrup. Good ol' Ben was also responsible for introducing tofu to the colonies. Yup, that's right—*tofu*. However, we'll forgive him for that because he did describe it as a cheese. If you think of tofu in that way, it seems a little more palatable (apologies to the tofu fans reading this; we're working on our aversion).

Franklin is also credited for making the potato a mainstream vegetable. Even the French deemed this root veggie poisonous (which is ironic, considering that we now call fried potatoes *French fries*). This prompted him to become an advocate for all foods from the colonies, and he often wrote of the New World's fantastic edible offerings.

As if we don't find Franklin and his love for food impressive enough, his sense of humor is even more remarkable. This is evident in a little story he wrote in 1780 called "Dialogue Between Franklin and the Gout." Enjoy.

> FRANKLIN: Eh! oh! eh! What have I done to merit these cruel sufferings?
> THE GOUT: Many things; you have ate and drank too freely, and too much indulged those legs of yours in their indolence.
> FRANKLIN: Who is it that accuses me?
> THE GOUT: It is I, even I, the Gout.
> FRANKLIN: What! my enemy in person?
> THE GOUT: [. . .] While the mornings are long, and you have leisure to go abroad, what do you do? Why, instead of gaining an appetite for breakfast, by salutary exercise, you amuse yourself with books, pamphlets, or newspapers, which commonly are not worth the reading. Yet you eat an inordinate breakfast, four dishes of tea, with cream, and one or two buttered toasts, with slices of hung beef, which I fancy are not things the most easily digested. Immediately afterwards you sit down to write at your desk, or converse with persons who apply to you on business. Thus the time passes till one, without any kind of bodily exercise.

Oh, Mr. Franklin, we don't exercise, either.

Ben Franklin's "Key" to a Good Sweet Potato Casserole

This is the wow *dish for your Thanksgiving table. The beautiful colors will highlight all of your favorite fall shades.*

INGREDIENTS

4½ cups chicken stock
3 sweet potatoes, peeled and thinly sliced
1 cup pecans, chopped finely
2 cups cranberries
¾ cup brown sugar
1 orange, zest and juice (about ¼ cup) (we used Cara cara oranges)
½ tsp salt
4 Tbsp maple syrup
1 tsp cinnamon
2 Tbsp apple cider vinegar
1 tsp ginger powder
½ tsp pepper
6 Tbsp unsalted butter, divided

DIRECTIONS

→ In a pot, bring the chicken stock and potatoes to a boil, cooking for 15 minutes. Remove from heat, drain, and set aside to cool in a large bowl.

→ Set oven to 425 degrees. In a mixing bowl, combine pecans, cranberries, brown sugar, orange zest, and orange juice. Stir, and set aside.

→ In a separate bowl, combine cooked potatoes, salt, maple syrup, cinnamon, apple cider vinegar, ginger powder, pepper, and 4 Tbsp melted butter. Toss in the bowl to cover all the potatoes and then place the mixture into a pie plate or baking dish. Evenly spread the potatoes in the pan.

→ Cover the potatoes evenly with the pecan mix. Add the remaining 2 Tbsp butter, cut into 4 pieces, on the top.

→ Cover the pretty casserole with aluminum foil and place in the oven for 30 minutes. Remove the foil and cook for another 20 minutes.

Coffee, Tea, or Chocolate?

Tea has always been a very British beverage, and it made its way to the colonies in the seventeenth century. As trade routes opened up and imports began to arrive along the East Coast, coffee and drinking chocolate became just as popular. As tradesmen come to the New World, tea, coffee, and chocolate pots were hand-forged and sold to some of the wealthier families. Chocolate pots were a bit different from coffee pots as there was an accommodation built in the lid for a stirring stick.

COFFEE

If you live in New England today, you know there is no shortage of coffee. More specifically, Dunkin' Donuts. Back in the 1600s, coffee was a luxury. Having coffee in your home was a status symbol. Having coffee in a coffee house was a bit more common, but it still didn't rival tea or ale as far as sales went. In the South, less fortunate folks and slaves invented substitute coffee (although they were forced to perform the painstaking task of grinding coffee beans, they were not permitted to drink it). A common substitute was made with burning cornmeal that was then boiled and sweetened with molasses.

TEA

Most of the tea consumed in the colonies was smuggled in due to the steep (ha, pun!) tax. The tax was first imposed in 1660, so along with the Stamp Act and import tax, all these additional costs to ship supplies just became too extravagant. This forced everyone to seek alternatives, giving rise to the popularity of coffee and chocolate.

CHOCOLATE

The Aztecs and Mayans are credited with harvesting cocoa beans and creating a beverage from their crops. In the colonies, a chocolate drink was more expensive than coffee, but it quickly became popular among high society. First, cocoa beans were formed into inedible bars. The bars were then grated into hot water, and sweeteners or spices were added for more flavor. Colonists believed that chocolate was a remedy for almost anything, and it was often sold at apothecaries. At one point, it was even believed to cure smallpox. Although we wholeheartedly believe that it certainly enhances our moods, early Americans had a false notion (damn it, why couldn't this be true?) that it also helped with weight loss.

More Beverages in the New World

After reading all this information about our forefathers' drinking habits, it is truly amazing to know that we survived. Especially when you consider all the alcoholic beverages consumed in those first two hundred years (and, uh, even now. Burp). Ale, rum, port, and Madeira wine were all the rage, and day drinking was practically required.

Fun little fact: Benjamin Franklin had many terms for being drunk: addled, afflicted, buzzey, etc. Our favorite is "Halfway to Concord." Another interesting (out of left field) tidbit: one of us lives near the town of Franklin, Massachusetts (named after Ben), where one of the most popular beverages is called a Franklin Wine Cooler. This bizarre drink consists of just red wine and orange soda. Sounds gross, but we dare you to try it.

Since colonial times, odd beverage combinations seem to have originated out of necessity, but they soon grew to be popular favorites in homes and taverns up and down the East Coast. Those who imbibed had to be clever and extremely creative in how they developed a wide array of adult beverages. Here are examples of some interesting adult beverages:

Syllabub: a bubbly and milky wine drink made with milk or cream. *Bub* was slang for "bubbly drink." Most versions call for a sweet dessert wine to be incorporated into the mixture.

Rattle-Skull: the term itself is slang for a chatty person, which is probably what happened after you drank it. The Rattle-Skull was a mixture of dark beer, rum, lime juice, and nutmeg.

The Flip: a beverage made with rum, beer, molasses, eggs, or cream (and sometimes dried pumpkin)—served hot in a ceramic mug.

Sangaree: a colonial version of Sangria, made with Madeira or port, lemon juice, sugar, and nutmeg.

Stone Fence: a delicious blend of hard cider and rum.

Whistlebelly: made popular in Salem, Massachusetts, the Whistlebelly, or Whistlebelly Vengeance, is made by simmering beer in a kettle and adding molasses and breadcrumbs.

The Birth of Our Nation!

We didn't get here without a fight.

The American Revolution took place between 1765 and 1783. The colonists rejected the authority of the King of Great Britain and his ability to tax them in the New World. What started out as protests evolved into a full-scale war, with the first shot being fired on April 19, 1775.

During the war, food was rationed. Soldiers were allowed one pound of bread, half a pound of beef or pork, one pint of milk, one quart of malt beer, a bit of peas or beans, some soap, and vinegar, if it was available. The quantities and staples varied over the years depending on the availability, but that was the standard set. Tough times. Long story short, we won, and on July 4, 1776, the Declaration of Independence was accepted. Voila! The United States was officially official—life, liberty, and the pursuit of happiness. Fifty-six people signed that declaration, but Thomas Jefferson was really the brains behind most of it.

Technically, July 4 wasn't made an official holiday until 1941, but celebrations to mark the birth of our independence date back to 1776. The earlier celebrations included mock funerals for the King, concerts, firing cannons, and parades. One could conclude that this also involved lots of food, which, as we know, has evolved into how we now celebrate—with cookouts and fireworks! Although our ancestors were not grilling burgers and dogs or drinking keg beer out of a red Solo cup, they did have special occasion meals (and beverages) that celebrated their new freedom. As of 1777, fireworks and picnics were directly tied to this holiday.

The word "picnic" originates from the French term *pique-nique* and is loosely defined as making a nice meal outside. Whereas it was mostly practiced by the upper class in Europe on their hunting and gaming trips, in the new United States, it was something *everyone* did, a community potluck event that brought neighbors of every social status outside to share food and drinks. Throw down a blanket and join us; we're bringing lobster, porridge, and sweet corn pudding to our *pique-nique*.

Exactly fifty years later, both Jefferson and John Adams died on the Fourth of July within hours of each other.

Liberty and Lobster for Everyone!

Lobster egg rolls with basil honey dipping sauce.

INGREDIENTS

Lobster:
2 Tbsp unsalted butter
3 cloves garlic, minced
1 lb lobster meat, cooked and chopped
2 Tbsp fresh chervil, finely chopped
1 Tbsp fresh tarragon, finely chopped
1 Tbsp fresh chive, finely chopped
½ cup cabbage, chopped into bite-size pieces
1 carrot, diced
Olive oil or butter
3 asparagus, sliced thin
1 tsp ground coriander
⅛ tsp salt
⅛ tsp pepper
Egg roll wrappers (you can find these in the
   produce section in the grocery store)
1 egg white
Vegetable oil

DIRECTIONS

Lobster:

➠ In a sauté pan, melt the butter on medium heat. Add garlic and fry until fragrant, but do not allow browning or, more important, burning. Add lobster meat, chervil, tarragon, and chives. Stir and cook for 1 or 2 minutes just to incorporate and to warm. Do not let the mixture cook too long as the lobster will become chewy if overcooked. Remove from heat, transfer lobster to a bowl, and set aside.

➠ In same pan, add the cabbage and carrots. Add a swirl of olive oil or pat of butter if the vegetables start to stick to the pan. Add the asparagus just as the cabbage and carrots begin to slightly soften. Asparagus cooks quickly and can become mushy. Yuck. Add the coriander, salt, and pepper. Remove from heat.

➠ Remove the egg roll wrappers from the refrigerator. We recommend having a damp towel on hand as you work with the wrappers. Egg roll wrappers, when stale or dry, can become difficult to work with and fall apart while frying. Covering the wrappers with the towel will prevent them from drying out. On a flat surface, brush the egg white on the outside edges of the egg roll wrapper. You will only need to do this to one side. Add equal parts lobster and vegetables to the bottom center of the wrapper closest to you. Fold the sides in snugly, and roll the wrappers. Seal the wrapper with another brush of egg white. These can be the day before, stored in your refrigerator, on a lined cookie sheet.

➠ Heat vegetable oil in a deep fry pan. You want to add enough oil to reach halfway up the lobster rolls. When the oil is hot, carefully place a few of the rolls in the frying pan. Work in batches as overcrowding affects the oil temperature. Using kitchen tongs, slightly lift the rolls to see if they are at the desired doneness. If so, turn to cook the other side.

➠ Do yourself a favor: let them cool for a few minutes or you will burn your mouth. Trust us. Serve with our Basil Honey Dipping Sauce (page 91).

INGREDIENTS

Basil Honey Dipping Sauce:

$1/3$ cup honey

2 Tbsp basil chiffonade (this is a fancy word for stacking the basil, rolling them tightly, and slicing it into long, thin strips)

2 Tbsp apple cider vinegar

1 Tbsp cornstarch

DIRECTIONS

Basil Honey Dipping Sauce:

↠ In a small saucepan on medium heat, combine honey, basil chiffonade, and apple cider vinegar, and stir. Gently sprinkle cornstarch while stirring, avoiding making any lumps. Cook for 2 minutes, and remove from heat. Strain the sauce, remove the basil, and set aside to cool and thicken. Dip away!

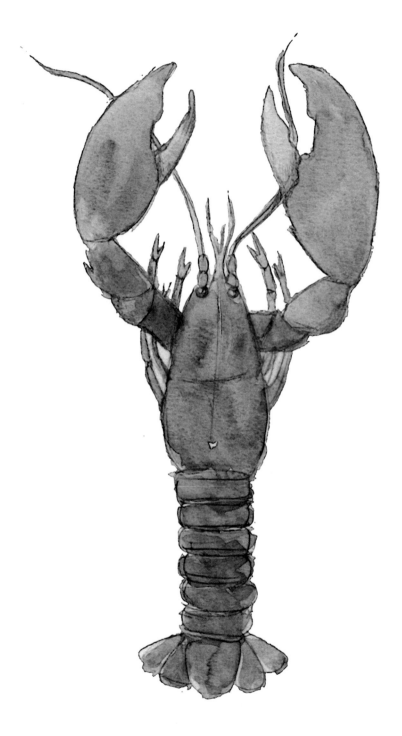

Warmed Mulled Apple Cider Sangria

While in Sweden, we met the loveliest couple, Peter and Fossy. They introduced us to the classic Nordic drink, glogg, which is delicious. We left Sweden with a love for this drink and wonderful new friends. This is our combination of the classic American mulled cider and Swedish glogg.

INGREDIENTS

1 bottle (750 ml) Cabernet Sauvignon
3½ cups apple cider
½ cup honey
½ cup apple brandy
1 apple, diced (we used an unpeeled Honeycrisp)
Zest of 1 orange, and large orange slices (we used Cara cara)
1 cup purple seedless grapes
½ cup currants
3 star anise
10 whole cloves
½ tsp nutmeg
½ tsp ginger powder
⅛ tsp ground cardamom
3 cinnamon sticks

DIRECTIONS

→ In a large sauce pan, add all the ingredients. Stir and cook on medium-low heat until hot. Serve the sangria with the drunken fruit and a cinnamon stick from the pan.

→ You can make this in advance, cover, and store in the refrigerator.

"Peace Porridge"

Pease porridge is a savory pudding or stew that usually involves some sort of boiled beans. We've added a bit of veal and other goodies to bring you a very comforting bowl of yummy.

INGREDIENTS

5 Tbsp all-purpose flour
2 tsp salt, divided, plus extra to taste
2 tsp white pepper, divided, plus extra to taste
1 tsp ground coriander
1 tsp allspice
1½ lb veal stew meat
4 Tbsp unsalted butter, divided
1 leek, trimmed, cleaned, and sliced
3 cloves garlic, minced
2 large carrots, peeled and sliced
2 parsnips, peeled and diced
1 turnip, peeled and diced
1 quart beef stock
2 cans (15 oz each) cannellini beans;
    reserve 1 Tbsp bean liquid; drain and rinse
    beans
3 pieces whole thyme

Pease porridge hot, pease porridge cold,
Pease porridge in the pot, nine days old;
Some like it hot, some like it cold,
Some like it in the pot, nine days old.

DIRECTIONS

➳ In a large plastic bag, combine flour, 1 tsp salt, 1 tsp white pepper, coriander, and allspice. Add the veal to the bag and coat all pieces with the flour mixture. Remove the flour-coated veal, set aside, and keep the bag of flour for later use.

➳ Heat 2 Tbsp butter in a Dutch oven on medium heat. Add the leeks and garlic, cook for 5 minutes, and then add the carrots, parsnips, and turnips. Sprinkle the remaining 1 tsp each of salt and pepper over the vegetables and cook until tender.

➳ Add the veal to the cooked vegetables, stir, and cook for 5 minutes.

➳ In a small bowl, melt the remaining 2 Tbsp butter and add the flour mixture from the plastic bag. Stir and add to the veal and vegetables. Cook for 3 minutes, while stirring to prevent burning.

➳ Pour 1 cup beef stock into the Dutch oven; stir to prevent the flour from becoming lumpy. Add the remaining stock to the pan.

➳ Raise the heat to medium-high, and cook until the liquid begins to boil. Add the beans, the reserved bean liquid, and thyme. Stir, and drop the heat to low.

➳ Simmer for 1½ hours. Salt and pepper to taste.

Bacon Croutons

Good with anything, but definitely throw some on top of that "Peace Porridge" (page 93).

INGREDIENTS

8 pieces cooked bacon, roughly chopped
2 cloves garlic
2 Tbsp fresh chives
2 Tbsp fresh tarragon
1 stick unsalted butter, melted
Salt, to taste
Pepper, to taste
1 loaf French bread, cut into bite-size pieces

DIRECTIONS

→ Set oven at 375 degrees. In a food processor, add bacon, garlic, chives, and tarragon. Blend until the ingredients are chopped into small bits. While processor is on, drizzle in the butter. Salt and pepper to taste.

→ In a mixing bowl, combine bread and bacon butter. Using your hands, spread the butter into the bread. Spread the butter-soaked bread on a lined sheet pan. Add any remaining bacon bits left in the mixing bowl to the bread on the pan.

→ Place the bread in the oven, tossing once or twice to ensure that all sides toast evenly. Bake for 15–20 minutes until browned. Remove from oven and cool.

→ Add bacon croutons to the top of a hot bowl of soup, preferably our "Peace Porridge" (page 93). Croutons taste great on salads, as well.

Corn and Clam Fritters

You may want to double this recipe—they are that good!

INGREDIENTS

1 Tbsp unsalted butter
2 cups minced clams, rinsed and drained
1 cup corn, preferably fresh (if you are using frozen corn, thaw and drain)
1 Tbsp fresh chervil, minced
½ cup beer (we used Stella Artois)
4 large eggs
2 cups self-rising flour
1½ tsp baking powder
½ tsp salt, plus extra to taste
Cooking oil or lard

DIRECTIONS

→ Melt the butter on medium heat in a sauté pan. Add the clams, corn, chervil, and beer. Cook for 4 minutes. Remove from heat, transfer to a mixing bowl, and cool.

→ Whisk eggs into the cooled clam mixture, followed by the flour, baking powder, and salt.

→ Heat a heavy pan—we suggest cast iron—on the stovetop at medium heat. Add your preferred cooking oil or fat to the pan. Make sure you have added enough oil for it to come up the sides of the fritter while it is cooking.

→ Scoop out 1 Tbsp of the fritter batter from the bowl and gently place it in the hot pan. Using the back of a wooden spoon, slightly flatten the fritter. If it is too thick, the center will not cook fully; if it is too thin, it will be too crispy. We suggest trying a test case, otherwise known as a sample (yum). Once the fritter has browned, turn it over and repeat.

→ Remove from heat and give the fritters a generous sprinkle of salt.

1769 Forefathers' Day

Forefathers' Day was celebrated on December 22, 1769, as created by the Old Colony Club. What started out as a memorial feast of gratitude for the country's founders evolved over the next fifty years into a political dinner with all the red tape. The Mayflower Society also celebrated this event.

LET US WEED OUT THE "UNSAVORIES"

The Old Colony Club consisted of a group of men who didn't like hanging around the "ungentlemanly folks" who frequented the local taverns. These men created a private club that weeded out any shady characters. Founded in 1769, it is one of the oldest gentlemen's clubs in the United States. The club members still meet to this day and continue their tradition of the Forefathers' Day feast, where top hats are required.

The Mayflower Society, as you may know, is a group that can certifiably trace their heritage to one of the original 102 settlers in Plimoth in 1620. It was founded in 1897. During this same time, many other groups that celebrated patriotism and heritage had started to form, such as the Daughters of the American Revolution. The Mayflower Society has chapters in all fifty states and continues to develop educational programs that highlight the crucial role the first settlers played in our history. If you're interested, get on one of those ancestry sites and trace your lineage. You could become a member of this prestigious society.

SUFFERIN' SUCCOTASH!

The celebratory but somewhat solemn meal of Forefathers' Day almost always included the dish known as succotash. Succotash traditionally contains corn, beans, and lard (and sometimes salt pork or corned beef). It dates back to 1751 and most likely came from the Algonquin Indians in Rhode Island. The name itself originates from the Narragansett Indian tribe's *sohquttahhash*, which translates to "broken pieces." While traditional succotash consists of all vegetables, Plimoth succotash was a special version served at the Forefathers' Day dinner. Instead of a medley of beans and corn, it was a broth containing chunks of game bird and/or meat that was sliced at the table. Ingredients included gray corned beef and salt pork, along with navy beans, potatoes, turnips, and hominy.

We are not entirely sure how the succotash of Forefathers' Day was established.

Praise Be to Cod

Cod en papillote with carrot and applejack coulis.

INGREDIENTS

Applejack Coulis:
2 Tbsp unsalted butter
1 onion, sliced
3 carrots, peeled and sliced
2 cups chicken stock
¼ tsp white pepper
½ tsp salt
½ tsp ground ginger
1 Tbsp Laird's Applejack
2 tsp apple cider vinegar

Cod:
2 Tbsp olive oil
1 clove garlic, minced
1 cup parsnips, peeled and diced
4 oz mushrooms (we used oyster mushrooms)
6 oz baby spinach
½–1 lb cod, cut into 4 pieces (depending on how
   large of a piece you would like)
Salt, to taste
White pepper, to taste

DIRECTIONS

Applejack Coulis:

➤ Melt butter in a sauté pan, on medium heat. Add onions and carrots, cooking until they are slightly tender.

➤ Add the chicken stock to the pan, and cook the vegetables until they are soft. Remove the pan from the stovetop and let cool slightly. Add sautéed vegetables and stock to a blender, working in batches. Blend the mixture until it resembles a thick soup.

➤ Set the burner to medium heat, and pour the mixture back into the pan. Add the white pepper, salt, ginger, applejack, and apple cider vinegar. Cook the mixture down until the liquid has reduced and the sauce is thick. Keep warm until you are ready to use.

Cod:

➤ Set the oven to 400 degrees.

➤ In a sauté pan, add the olive oil and warm. Add the garlic, followed immediately by the parsnips. Once the parsnips begin to soften, add the mushrooms, and cook until they soften. Add the spinach, and continue to stir until the spinach wilts. Remove from heat and set aside.

➤ Tear off 4 pieces of parchment paper and set in front of you. Evenly spread the mushroom and parsnip mix in the middle of each piece of parchment. Place a filet of cod over each vegetable mixture. Salt and pepper to taste. You can also add a small amount of the coulis on top, but save enough for serving.

➤ There are certainly more fancy ways to folding the parchment, en papillote, but a solid fold and seal will work just fine. We take two sides of the parchment, meet the edges in the air over the fish, and roll down until the parchment just about touches the fish. Then, fold the sides under the fish. Place the fish packets on a shallow baking pan and cook for 30 minutes.

➤ Remove the packets from the oven. Evenly spoon the coulis on the plates. Using a spatula, lift up the vegetables and fish from the parchment, and place on the coulis. Discard the parchment. Serve.

Sufferin' Succotash with a Luxury Topping

(Ahem . . . lobster). Of course, you can enjoy the succotash as a side, or you can layer the vegetables with a crispy polenta cake and buttered lobster. Yes, please.

INGREDIENTS

Polenta Cake:
1 cup whole milk
$2/3$ cup heavy cream
2 Tbsp unsalted butter
$1/3$ cup cornmeal, packed
$1\frac{1}{2}$ Tbsp grated cheese (we used Parmesan)
$1/8$ tsp pepper
$1/4$ tsp salt
1 Tbsp fresh sage, minced (about 4 leaves)
Olive oil

Succotash:
1 can (15 oz) cannellini beans (reserve the liquid
   in the can for later), rinse and drain the beans
3 tsp fresh lemon juice
3 Tbsp unsalted butter
2 shallots ($1/4$ cup), thinly sliced
2 cups fennel, trimmed and cut into small pieces
1 leek, white portion (approximately $1\frac{1}{2}$ cups),
   cleaned and trimmed
1 tsp salt
$1/2$ tsp white pepper
2 garlic cloves, minced
2 cups fresh raw corn
Zest from 1 lemon
2 tsp chervil, thinly chopped

Buttered Lobster:
1 stick unsalted butter, divided and cut into 8 tablespoons
1 Tbsp water
1 clove garlic, minced
$1/2$ lb raw lobster tail meat, cut into chunks
6 large raw shrimp, rinsed, deveined, and minced
Salt, to taste
White pepper, to taste

To Asemble:
Herbs, to garnish, e.g., parsley or tarragon (optional)

DIRECTIONS

Polenta Cake:

➤ Combine all the ingredients for the polenta, except for the olive oil, in a cold saucepan. Turn the heat on to medium, stir, and cook until the mixture becomes thick. As you are stirring, you will notice the cornmeal start to move away from the sides of the pan. That is usually a good indicator that it is done. Remove the pan from the heat, and let it cool for 3–5 minutes.

- Lay a piece of parchment paper on a flat surface. Pour the cooled cornmeal onto the parchment; it will have a consistency of mashed potatoes. Let it cool on the parchment for a few minutes. As it cools, you will notice the cornmeal thickening to a consistency that can be molded. Using the parchment, mold the mixture into a tube. Make the tube in any size you want, but note that this will go into the refrigerator and remain at that size. Wrap the tube in plastic wrap and chill in the refrigerator for at least 1 hour.

- Remove the tube from the refrigerator, and cut ½-inch rounds from the batter. Heat a heavy pan on medium heat with olive oil. Once the pan is hot, add the rounds and cook until brown. Flip to the other side and repeat.

Succotash:

- In a small bowl, combine the bean liquid and lemon juice, and set aside.

- Melt the butter in a sauté pan, over medium heat. Add the shallots, fennel, leeks, salt, and pepper, and cook until the vegetables become tender and lightly brown, about 5 minutes. Add the garlic, stir, and cook for another 1 minute.

- Add the beans and corn to the sauté pan with the vegetables. You will not need to cook this for long, maybe 3–4 minutes. Add the lemon bean liquid and stir, followed by lemon zest and chervil.

Buttered Lobster:

- On medium heat, add the butter, water, and garlic to a sauté pan. Stir until the butter has melted. You will notice that the water will emulsify the butter and create a sauce.

- Add the lobster and shrimp, and cook until the meat is no longer translucent. This should take a few minutes. Do not overcook the lobster as it will become chewy. Salt and pepper to taste.

To Assemble:

- Place a polenta cake on a plate with a scoop of the succotash, followed by the butter lobster. Optional: add a sprinkling of fresh herbs, like parsley or tarragon, on top. Though there are a number of steps, this recipe is quite easy and the results are delicious.

Savory Cranberry Bread Pudding

Sweet and savory, tart and complex, this little side dish can stand on its on. The flavors are beautiful alone or served with a ham or turkey.

INGREDIENTS

½ loaf French bread, cut into bite-size pieces (about 4 cups)
7 Tbsp unsalted butter, divided
3 sprigs fresh thyme; remove leaves and leave them whole, not chopped
Salt, to taste
Pepper to taste
1½ cups chicken stock, divided
2 cups whole cranberries (Fresh are preferred, but we find that frozen whole cranberries are delicious during the off seasons. If you use frozen, make sure they are completely thawed.)
¾ cup sugar
½ tsp salt
½ tsp cinnamon

DIRECTIONS

→ Set oven to 400 degrees.

→ Add the bread, 4 Tbsp melted butter, and thyme leaves in a bowl. Combine, and add salt and pepper to taste. Spread the mixture on a baking sheet, and toast until golden. Immediately remove from the oven and cool.

→ Once the bread is cool, put in a sealable container, and add 1 cup chicken stock. Seal the container and shake, making sure all pieces are mixed up in the stock. Store in the refrigerator for at least a few hours or until the entire mixture has soaked up stock. This can be done the day before.

→ Start the cranberry puree. In a saucepan, combine 1 Tbsp butter, cranberries, and ½ cup chicken stock. Cook until the cranberries are soft and plump. You may need to lower the heat to medium to prevent the puree from burning.

→ Once your puree mixture is cooked, pour into a fine mesh sieve held over another bowl. Using a plastic spatula, gently push the cranberries through the sieve. Since the mixture is thick, most of the puree will be stuck on the outside bottom of the sieve. Use your spatula to get the puree off the sieve and into the bowl. Continue to push the cranberries through until you notice there is no liquid left, and all that remains is pulp and skin.

→ Set the oven to 350 degrees.

→ Wipe the original saucepan down with a paper towel, and return your cranberry puree to the pan. Add the sugar, ½ tsp salt, cinnamon, and the remaining 2 Tbsp butter. Stir frequently, and cook until the butter is melted and the sugar is absorbed into the mixture. Remove from the heat.

→ Take your bread out of the refrigerator and stir it into the cranberry mixture. Use the plastic spatula to stir and lightly press into the bread, making sure the cranberry puree gets absorbed.

→ Add the cranberry mixture to 4 ramekins or a larger oven-safe bowl (extend your cooking time for the latter). Place in the oven for 40 minutes or until the top starts to get dark and crispy.

Oldest Food Brands in North America!

You've most likely heard of these brands but probably don't know how long they've been around. Through thick and thin, these companies have withstood the test of time. In this chapter, we've developed some fun recipes highlighting their famous products.

1764, Baker's Chocolate

In 1764, John Hannon and Dr. James Baker began their chocolate company in Dorchester, Massachusetts. They imported beans from the West Indies and developed "drinking chocolate" that was sold as a sort of cake or disk. In 1804, Dr. Baker's son took over the business and began growing the product lines and increasing production, as well as distribution. By 1852, Baker's Chocolate was a staple in almost every household.

Decadent White Chocolate Rice Pudding

The tender rice pudding is lightly scented with cardamom and enhanced with a kiss of white chocolate. Decadent, indeed.

INGREDIENTS

½ cup heavy cream
1½ cups whole milk
¼ cup sugar
¾ tsp ground cardamom
½ cup Arborio rice
4 oz white chocolate, chopped into small pieces

DIRECTIONS

⇥ Heat the cream, milk, sugar, and cardamom in a small stockpot on medium-high heat. Once the milk reaches the boiling point, add the rice. Stir, and drop the temperature down to a simmer and cover. Stir every so often to ensure the rice is not burning or sticking to the bottom. Cooking takes about 30 minutes. You are ready to proceed to the next step once most of the liquid has evaporated but there is still some left, keeping the rice creamy.

⇥ Stir the chocolate into the rice mixture. The chocolate will melt quickly. Remove from the heat. We poured the rice pudding into two glass jam jars.

⇥ Cool and devour.

1780, Laird & Company

Laird & Company is the oldest licensed distillery in the United States. It was established in 1780 in Colts Neck Township, New Jersey, by Robert Laird. Robert served in the Revolutionary War under George Washington, and it is reported that George wrote to the Laird family prior to the war asking for the family recipe for their applejack. At the time, apples were one of the most abundant crops in the colonies, so it only made sense to produce a cider spirit. Applejack is still quite popular, and we've found a delicious way to cook with it.

Applejack Crisp Pie

If the colonists had this recipe, there would be no applejack left to drink. One bite and you might forget all about your grandma's apple pie recipe. Sorry, Grandma.

INGREDIENTS

Crisp:
1 stick cold, unsalted butter, plus 1 Tbsp butter
¼ cup sliced almonds
1 cup all-purpose flour
½ cup brown sugar, packed
1 tsp cinnamon
¼ tsp salt

Pie:
3 Tbsp unsalted butter, melted (plus extra to
    grease the pan)
Piecrust (store-bought or made using your
    favorite recipe)
½ cup brown sugar, packed
¼ cup sugar
1 Tbsp cornstarch
½ tsp cinnamon
½ tsp ground ginger
¼ tsp nutmeg
¼ tsp salt
5 apples, peeled, cored, and sliced thin (we used
    Granny Smith)
¼ cup Laird's Applejack

DIRECTIONS

Crisp:

↠ To make the crisp, melt 1 Tbsp butter in a small pan. Add the sliced almonds and toast until brown but *not* burnt. Immediately remove from heat. In a food processor, combine the flour, brown sugar, cinnamon, salt, and almonds. Pulse until the almonds are pea-sized. Quickly break the stick of butter in half and throw into the food processor. Pulse until incorporated. Chill until you are ready to use.

Pie:

↠ Set the oven to 400 degrees. Butter a deep-dish pie pan and line with your piecrust.

↠ In a large mixing bowl, combine brown sugar, white sugar, cornstarch, cinnamon, ginger, nutmeg, and salt. Once fully mixed, add apples, melted butter, and applejack. Gently stir, fully coating each piece of apple. Pour the apple mixture onto your piecrust.

↠ Cover apple pie with the chilled crisp, gently pressing down onto the crisp. Place the pie plate on a shallow baking pan, to prevent any spillage. Cook for 50 minutes, or until golden.

1790, King Arthur Flour

Originally known as Sands, Taylor & Wood Company, King Arthur Flour has been in business since 1790. Henry Wood supplied the colonies with flour, mixes, and cookbooks, quickly becoming a very successful and respected brand with his customers—and it still is today. We've used King Arthur Flour in these recipes.

1795, Jim Beam

The Bohm family came from Germany and settled in Kentucky. Soon after, they changed their name to Beam and began producing a whiskey (bourbon) originally called Old Jake Beam Sour Mash. The corn grown in western Pennsylvania and Kentucky created a sweet and flavorful whiskey that quickly became famous, generating a high demand. By 1830, Jim Beam was shipping their product in used fish and vinegar barrels. Sounds gross, but by burning those barrels, they created the perfect smoky storage for what is now known as a Kentucky bourbon.

Bourbon Oatmeal Raisin Cookies

This recipe is so simple, and you will not need a stand mixer.

INGREDIENTS

1½ cups raisins

⅓ cup good quality bourbon, plus a little extra to taste (We used Jim Beam. To make the best cookie, do not use inexpensive bourbon that you would not drink.)

1½ stick butter, melted

¾ cup brown sugar, packed

½ cup sugar

½ tsp cinnamon

1 large egg and 1 large yolk, beaten together

1 Tbsp molasses

1 tsp vanilla

½ tsp baking soda

¾ tsp salt

1 cup all-purpose flour

3 cups old-fashioned oats

DIRECTIONS

↬ Combine the raisins and bourbon in a bowl, and set aside for at least 30 minutes.

↬ In a large mixing bowl, combine the butter, brown sugar, white sugar, and cinnamon. Stir well. Add the eggs, and mix well. Add the molasses and vanilla.

↬ Now, add the dry ingredients, one at a time, starting with the baking soda and salt, then the flour, followed by the oats.

↬ After all the ingredients are well-mixed, add the bourbon-soaked raisins, along with any remaining liquid in the bowl. Stir. (Trust us, do not start eating the batter—you will not have any left).

↬ Cover the bowl with plastic wrap and pop it in the refrigerator until chilled, about 1 hour.

↬ Heat oven to 375 degrees. Prepare your cookies on a lined baking tray (we use Silpat). We suggest making them into balls, and then flattening them slightly with your hands or the back of a spoon. Cook until golden. Depending on size of the cookie, cook for 12–17 minutes.

Washington's Wine

The man liked his Madeira.

Madeira is a particular wine, very similar to port wine, that is produced on the island of Madeira. Madeira is a Portuguese island that in fact sits closer to Morocco. If you ever get the chance to visit, stay in Reid's Palace in Funchal. It's spectacular. And definitely pick up a bottle (ahem, or a case) of Madeira wine.

President George Washington had a fondness for Madeira, so much so that he ordered 126 gallons of it in 1759. George even ordered a second 126 gallons well before he finished the first. He went on to place five more orders during his political career and was particularly demanding that it be a good vintage. At the White House, it was served during the fruit and nut course of special dinners and was often brought back out again during the after-dinner discussion, when it was reported that the president always ended the night with three full glasses. Thomas Jefferson was also a big fan of Madeira wine. It just so happens that the men signing the Declaration of Independence were drinking Madeira as they put their (haha) John Hancock on the parchment.

Madeira ranges from dry to sweet and is usually served with dessert. Madeira island has a rich history of making wine that dates as far back as the fifteenth century. The making of Madeira wine is unique in that involves a heating process. This process was discovered when orders for the wine were exported and delivered by ship—heating and cooling temperatures during travel, along with constant movement, affected the taste in a way that became not just favorable; it was now in demand. Today, stainless steel vats are heated using a water process over a period of no less than three months to create the same taste.

There are several types of Madeira. These include:

Sercial: lemony, spicy, sweet, and more of an aperitif. Served chilled.
Verdelho: smoky, concentrated, and rich. An intense version that is more flexible with different dishes.
Boal: sweet, complex, aromatic. Best for desserts or nuts.
Malmsey: the richest and sweetest of the bunch. It is a dessert on its own.

It's also incredibly rewarding and delicious to cook with. We used many, many bottles of Madeira in the making of this book, and as Julia Child would say, some of it went into the dishes.

Beef for the chief

Herb-crusted filet of beef topped with sweet wine reduction.

INGREDIENTS

Herbed Crust:
9 Tbsp unsalted butter, cut into tablespoons at
    room temperature, divided
1 cup panko
2 Tbsp parsley, minced
Rosemary, 2 tsp minced
¼ tsp salt
2 cloves garlic, minced

Beef:
1 cup Madeira wine
½ cup balsamic vinegar
3 Tbsp sugar
4 filet mignons
Sea salt, to taste
Freshly ground pepper, to taste
2 Tbsp olive oil
Rosemary, 2 whole sprigs
2 cloves garlic, smashed

DIRECTIONS

Herbed Crust:

❊ Make the herbed crust. Keep in mind that you will eventually be using the crust for your steak. The recipe for herbed crust makes more than what you will need for this dish, so you will have leftover crust for the next time you need a quick flavor boost for a meal. There are many uses for herbed crust, for example, adding a flavorful layer to meat, chicken, and fish. Melt 1 Tbsp butter in a sauté pan on medium heat. Once the butter is melted, add the panko, parsley, 2 tsp minced rosemary, salt, and 2 cloves minced garlic to the pan. Cook until the all the ingredients are blended and the panko begins to toast. Remove from heat.

❊ In a mixing bowl, combine the toasted panko and the remaining 8 Tbsp butter until fully mixed. Using your hands works best, so rings off, chefs; you will spend much time cleaning your rings if you do not take them off.

❊ Prepare a baking pan (that can fit into your freezer) and 2 pieces of parchment paper of the same size. Lay a single piece of parchment on a flat surface and add the panko mixture on top, spreading evenly. Lay the second piece of parchment paper on top. Using a rolling pin, flatten the panko layer into a ¼ inch. Try to keep the mixture in a size no bigger than the pan; ours was the size of a standard piece of paper. Carefully pick the 2 pieces of parchment up and lay it on your baking pan. Pop it into the freezer for a quick freeze.

Beef:

- Make the Madeira reduction. On the stovetop, add the Madeira wine and balsamic vinegar on medium heat. Cook until it reduces down by half. Add the sugar and stir. Continue to cook until the mixture coats the back of your spoon and becomes syrup, 5–7 minutes. Keep on simmering until you are ready to use.

- This next section is all about timing and being prepared. Filet mignon is expensive and lean, and overcooking can happen very quickly, which could take the meal from great to okay to, well, that was a waste.

- Set your oven to 425 degrees. Remove the meat from the refrigerator at least 20 minutes before you start cooking. The perfect cooked filet is one that, when you cut into it, will look the same from edge to center. Allowing it get to room temperature helps you achieve that goal. Generously season the meat with sea salt and pepper. We prefer to add about 1/8 tsp salt and pepper to each side. We also recommend tying kitchen string around the outside of the filet for even cooking.

- In a heavy oven-safe pan (cast iron is really the best), heat the olive oil on medium-high heat until it is very hot (hint: turn that kitchen fan on and perhaps open a window). Gently lay each filet down on the pan and listen to it sear. In the pan, add 2 sprigs rosemary and 2 cloves smashed garlic. The flavors will gently infuse into your meat. Cook the meat for 4 undisturbed minutes. Use a timer so you do not overcook the side.

- While that is cooking, remove the herbed crust from the freezer, and, through the parchment, cut out a size that will fit your steak. The herbed crust will be frozen and easy to cut through. Remove the parchment paper. Flip the filet over, and add the herbed crust to the top of the steak. Move the pan to the oven and cook for 5–7 minutes; 5 minutes for rare, 6 minutes for medium-rare, or 7 minutes for medium. In the meantime, cut the remaining herbed crust into steak-size pieces, place in a freezer-safe bag, and pop back in the freezer for future use.

- Remove meat from the oven (careful, do not burn yourself). Remove the steak from the pan and trim off the string. Allow the meat to rest for a few minutes; you can also cover loosely with foil.

- Swirl a few spoonfuls of Madeira balsamic reduction on a plate and lay that beautiful herb-crusted filet on top.

The Rest of the Story: Fun Food Facts and Delicious History

Presidential Foodie Favorites

Comfort food is defined as food that provides consolation or a feeling of well-being, often associated with childhood. These presidential favorites are well-documented, and although ice cream seems to be a favorite with most of them, squirrel stew is one of the more unusual dishes to feature. Squirrel meat is described as tasting like a cross between duck and lamb—we'll take their word for it.

George Washington: Fish and ice cream

John Adams: Indian pudding

Thomas Jefferson: French food, ice cream

James Madison: Ice cream

James Monroe: Fried chicken

John Quincy Adams: Fresh fruit

Andrew Jackson: French food

Martin Van Buren: Oysters, donuts

William Henry Harrison: Squirrel stew

John Tyler: Pudding

James K. Polk: Cornpone

Zachary Taylor: Creole food, spicy food

Millard Fillmore: Soup (Fillmore was the first to install a cast-iron stove in the White House.)

Franklin Pierce: Fried clams

James Buchanan: Fresh butter

Abraham Lincoln: Chicken fricassee, herbed biscuits

Alexander Hamilton: Beef, anything with apples

Source: Blankenship, Sara, "The Favorite Foods of All 44 Presidents," *Dallas Observer*, Feb 20, 2012.

MARTIN VAN BUREN

Hard Cider Glazed Donuts

Don't try to pretend you don't want to eat them all. It happens. The donuts are best served warm.

INGREDIENTS

2 packets (¼ oz) yeast
¼ cup hard cider (slightly warmed for donuts),
   plus ½ cup for glaze
1 cup light cream
½ cup 2% milk
1 stick unsalted butter
½ cup sugar
2 large eggs
1 tsp vanilla paste
5 cups self-rising flour, plus extra for dusting
2 cups confectioners' sugar
Cooking oil

DIRECTIONS

❧ Combine the yeast and ¼ cup warm hard cider in a standing mixer with a hook paddle. Let the mixture sit for 15 minutes. You will notice the mixture becomes frothy.

❧ While the yeast is setting, heat the cream, milk, and butter on medium heat until small bubbles begin to form, but do not boil. Turn the heat off and let it cool slightly.

❧ In the mixing bowl with yeast, set the mixer on a low speed and add the sugar, eggs (one at a time), and vanilla paste. Slowly add 1 Tbsp at a time of the warmed milk mixture to the mixer (careful not to cook the eggs) until the temperature of the mixture rises. Then, pour the remaining milk mixture into the mixer.

❧ Slowly add the flour, scraping down the sides. Speed up the mixer slightly and continue mixing until the dough starts to form a ball. Stop the mixer, and remove the hook paddle. Dampen a kitchen towel with warm water and place it over the dough. Let sit for 1 hour in a draft-free location.

❧ Remove the dough from the bowl and place on a flat, floured surface. Time to make the donuts. Using a rolling pin and a dusting of flour, flatten out the dough until it is about 1/2 inch thick. Using a kitchen glass or biscuit cutter, create rounds. We used a cupcake cutter to create the center hole, but you can use anything small and round, like an apple corer. Place parchment paper (or a Silpat) on a cookie sheet and lay the rounds on the paper. Chill the dough in the refrigerator for 20 minutes.

* Create the glaze by combining ½ cup hard cider and confectioners' sugar in a shallow bowl.

* Add cooking oil to a deep pan. There should be enough to allow the dough to float (a few inches). Heat the oil on medium until it reaches about 350 degrees. Add the chilled dough to the oil; be careful not to overcrowd the pan. The donuts will start to puff up. Once you see the cooking side of the donut start to brown, gently flip to the other side. This happens quickly, so watch the pan.

* Remove the donut from the hot oil and add it to the glaze, turning to coat all sides. Place the donut on a cookie rack to cool. Consider placing a plate or vessel underneath the rack, as the glaze will drip.

Liberating Chicken Fricassee with Skillet Cornmeal Biscuits

An honest tribute to the Great Emancipator. Good Old Abe loved his chicken fricassee! Fricassee involves cooking cut-up meat that is braised or sauteed and serving it with a white sauce. This French term dates back to the mid-sixteenth century and is thought to be a combination of the words frire *(to fry) and* casser *(to break into pieces.) Julia Child referred to it as "halfway between a saute and a stew."*

INGREDIENTS

Chicken Fricassee

3 lb chicken thighs, boneless and trimmed
1 tsp salt
1 tsp pepper
½ cup all-purpose flour, plus 2 Tbsp extra
4 Tbsp unsalted butter, divided
2 Tbsp olive oil
2 sprigs fresh thyme
2 carrots, peeled and julienned
2 stalks celery, diced finely
1 onion, thinly sliced
1 cup white wine (we used Riesling)
4 cups chicken stock
2 bay leaves
¼ tsp nutmeg
2 egg yolks, whisked
¼ cup heavy cream
6 oz baby spinach
2 Tbsp fresh lemon juice
1 Tsp tarragon
Salt, to taste
Pepper, to taste

DIRECTIONS

Chicken Fricassee:

➔ In a large plastic bag, add the chicken, salt, pepper, and ½ cup flour. Seal the bag and shake, covering each piece of chicken with the flour.

➔ Heat 2 Tbsp butter and olive oil in a deep pan or Dutch oven on medium-high. Add the whole fresh sprigs of thyme to the pan. Remove each piece of chicken from the bag, shaking off any excess flour, and discard the bag of flour. Add the chicken to the hot pan, working in batches. Cook until both sides are brown, and remove from the pan. Set aside.

➔ Add the carrots, celery, and onions to the pan until they begin to become soft. Add the remaining 2 Tbsp butter, melt, and add the remaining 2 Tbsp flour to the pan. Stir for 3 minutes until the flour soaks up all the liquid.

➔ Add the wine to the pan, and stir well. Continue to cook and stir the vegetables and wine until the mixture is thick and the liquid is gone. Add the chicken stock and bay leaves, stirring well to ensure there are no lumps. Turn the heat up to medium-high, and bring the liquid to a boil. Add the nutmeg, stir, and return the chicken to the pan. Lower the heat to simmer and lightly cover the pan. Cook for 20 minutes.

- While the chicken is cooking, combine the egg yolks and cream in a small bowl.

- Uncover the pan, remove bay leaves, add the spinach, and stir.

- Remove 1 tsp of the liquid from the pan and slowly add it to the egg mix while stirring, to temper the eggs. Repeat that step three more times, raising the temperature of the eggs. Slowly drizzle the warmed egg mixture into the pan with the chicken.

- Finish with the lemon juice, tarragon, and salt and pepper to taste. Suggestion: serve with our Skillet Cornmeal Biscuits (see below).

INGREDIENTS

Skillet Cornmeal Biscuits:

3½ cups self-rising flour, plus extra for dusting
½ cup cornmeal
1 Tbsp sugar
2 tsp salt
1 stick unsalted butter (frozen), plus 3 Tbsp
   (room temperature), divided
2 cups buttermilk, cold

DIRECTIONS

Skillet Cornmeal Biscuits:

- Heat the oven at 425 degrees.

- In a large mixing bowl, combine the flour, cornmeal, sugar, and salt. Remove 1 stick butter from the freezer. Using a cheese grater, shred the butter over the flour. We hold the butter with a clean dishcloth or paper towel. The butter is the reason you get delicious layers. The warmer the butter gets with your touch, the less effective it becomes. Use a wooden spoon or pastry cutter to blend the butter into the flour. This should not look fully combined; there will be flour-covered butter balls in the bowl.

- Add the buttermilk and stir. Do not over-handle this dough. It should not look smooth like pizza or bread dough; instead, it should look like it does not want to fully stick together. If you think it is too dry, add a bit more buttermilk.

- Place a cast-iron skillet into the oven to get it piping hot! We used a 12-inch cast-iron skillet. Helpful hint: have a good pair of oven mitts available.

- Invert the bowl of dough over a lightly floured surface. Using your hands, not a rolling pin, shape the dough while flattening it a bit. Remember: do not overdo it with your hands. The dough should be about 1-inch thick. Keep working with the dough until there is nothing left, reforming as needed. Using a large biscuit cutter makes about 10–12 biscuits.

- Open the oven, and drop 2 Tbsp butter into the skillet. Once melted, add the biscuits to the pan. The biscuits should be touching each other and fill up the pan. We melted an additional 1 Tbsp butter and basted the top.

- Cook for 15–17 minutes, or until the biscuits become nice and golden.

- Serve with our Cranberry and Orange Honey Butter (page 50) or use them to sop up the Liberating Chicken Fricassee (page 115). These are so easy to make and so delicious that you will find reasons to make them!

Beef Stew with Apple Brandy

A dedication to Hamilton's mother, who supported their family by running a provisions shop that sold apples.

INGREDIENTS

5 Tbsp all-purpose flour
1 Tbsp cornstarch
2 tsp salt
1 tsp pepper
2½ lb chuck roast, cut into bite-size pieces
2 Tbsp olive oil, plus a little extra
2 cups onions, diced (we used sweet onions)
1 carrot, peeled and diced
1 apple, peeled, cored, and diced
½ cup apple brandy
2½ cups apple cider
¾ cup water
¼ cup apple cider vinegar
2 bay leaves
Salt, to taste
Pepper, to taste

DIRECTIONS

→ In large plastic bag, combine flour, cornstarch, salt, and pepper. Working in batches, add the pieces of meat into the bag, seal, and shake to cover each piece of meat. Remove the meat and shake the excess flour back into the bag. Set aside and repeat. Discard the bag and its contents.

→ Heat a Dutch oven on medium-high. Add 2 Tbsp olive oil. Once the olive oil heats up, working in batches, add the meat to the pan and brown. Once the meat browns, remove from the pan and place on plate lined with paper towels.

→ Add the onions and carrots, and cook until soft. You may need to add a bit more olive oil to prevent burning at the bottom of the pan. Once the onions and carrots are ready, add the apple and stir. Cook for 2 minutes.

→ Add the apple brandy, and scrape up the beautiful brown bits from the bottom of the pan. Add the apple cider, water, and apple cider vinegar. Stir. Return the meat to the pan, and add the bay leaves. Increase the heat to medium-high until the liquid boils. Cover, lower the heat to low, and simmer for 2 hours.

→ Remove bay leaves. Salt and pepper to taste. As with most soup, this tastes best the next day.

Andouille and Shrimp Hush Puppies

Nothing to hush about, these are delicious and perfect for sharing.

INGREDIENTS

1½ cups andouille sausage, diced
2 Tbsp unsalted butter
2 cloves garlic, minced
1 cup shrimp, minced
1 Tbsp fresh tarragon, finely chopped
¼ tsp Old Bay seasoning
2 cups cornmeal
1¾ Tbsp self-rising flour
1 tsp baking powder
1 tsp baking soda
1 tsp salt
½ cup white onion, grated and drained of
   moisture
2 cups buttermilk
1 egg, beaten
Lard or high-heat cooking oil

DIRECTIONS

➤ Cook andouille sausage on the stovetop until browned. Remove from heat and set aside in a mixing bowl.

➤ Using the same pan, melt the butter on medium-low heat. Add the garlic and cook until fragrant. Add the shrimp to the pan and cook until it is no longer translucent; however, it should still not be fully cooked. Sprinkle in the tarragon and Old Bay seasoning. Stir and remove from heat.

➤ In a mixing bowl, combine the cornmeal, flour, baking powder, baking soda, and salt. Stir. Add the onions and stir well.

➤ In the bowl with the sausage, combine the shrimp, buttermilk, and egg. Stir to combine. Slowly whisk, to avoid creating lumps, the sausage mixture into the dry ingredients until everything is fully combined.

➤ When you are ready to cook the hush puppies, drop a big spoonful of lard or oil into a deep fry pan on medium heat. Ideally, you want the cooking oil to go halfway up the hush puppy. Start with a sample hush puppy. Dip a spoon into cold water, take a spoonful of the batter, and add it to the fat. Remember: you want the hush puppy to be big enough to eat in two bites, but not so big that the outside burns while the inside is still uncooked. Keep a keen eye on this as you do not want your hush puppy to burn. Once you test out your first sample, you will be able to determine how long to cook the rest. Adjust your temperature as needed.

Polly Want a Quaker?

Eat and drink in moderation, but indulge from time to time in your new friend Cream Cheese.

The Quakers, also known as the Society of Friends, mostly settled in New England and some of the middle colonies. They weren't welcome in the South due to their civil disobedience (they spoke up and questioned authority). Those of stricter religious backgrounds viewed them as a threat. But the Quakers were peaceful people, tired of religious intolerance. Even in the New World, they were somewhat persecuted (or rather made to feel unwelcome and labeled as "heretics"). Eventually, they seemed to thrive in Pennsylvania and the Delaware Valley. As a humble but outspoken group, they were the first to come out against slavery, view women as spiritually equal to men (unlike most religious institutions at the time), build schools and universities, and develop education programs for Native Americans.

As far as food goes, the Quakers were strict with diet. Overindulging was strongly discouraged. They did not eat butter (it was tainted by sin—see you in hell, Paula Dean), and they stuck with plain and simple dishes despite the wide array of new ingredients found in this new land. They also did not drink coffee because it was produced by slave labor. Boiling was the preferred method of cooking—almost every meal was boiled. Dumplings were their main dish, but they also ate dried meats, which they also used to flavor dumplings. In fact, they used dried meats in so many dishes it was often referred to as "Quaker gravy." On a more interesting note, the Quakers are credited as inventing cream cheese and scrapple. While you most certainly have heard of cream cheese, scrapple is a pudding made from scraps of meat and various grains, and it is still popular in certain parts of Pennsylvania.

LET'S GO DUTCH

Dutch Americans, mostly located in New Netherland—now called New York—had a more interesting diet. I think we owe these settlers a big thank you for introducing us to cookies and waffles! They were incredibly social and gathered regularly to dance, celebrate their heritage, drink, smoke, and just be friendly to one another. They were big on community and everything to do with food. As you may have guessed, they also brought us the Dutch oven. As big foodies, the Dutch took great care into food preparation. These specific pots allowed for slow, steady cooking and produced what we now call a casserole.

The Dutch were well-known for having a sweet tooth (or teeth) and, along with cookies and waffles, they also brought with them *olykoek*, a deep fried ball of dough with apples and raisins—heaven. During the holidays, it was common to see fancy pastries covered in almond paste alongside the traditional plates of meat and vegetable casseroles, cabbage dishes, pea and bean spreads, dried cod, and fish soups.

We've combined the Quaker's love of cream cheese with a celebratory bourbon sauce as a nod to the Dutch and strongly recommend you pair said cheesecake with the Fish House Punch (page 125).

Quaker Baker Cheesecake in an Apple with Decadent Dutch Bourbon Sauce

An incredibly easy-to-make dessert that will impress your guests. Try not to consume all of the bourbon sauce before your guests arrive.

INGREDIENTS

Cheesecake:
8 apples (we used Granny Smith)
3 Tbsp unsalted butter
1 Tbsp brown sugar
1 tsp cinnamon, plus extra to sprinkle
16 oz cream cheese, room temperature
1 cup sugar
3 large eggs
1 tsp vanilla paste
½ cup Biscoff cookies, crushed (you can also use graham crackers)

Bourbon Caramel Sauce:
7 oz (200 g) sugar
1½ stick cold butter, cut into pats
10.5 oz (300 ml) heavy cream
2 Tbsp bourbon (we used Jim Beam)*
⅛ tsp sea salt

*TIP
2 Tbsp bourbon will give it a light bourbon flavor. Add another 1 Tbsp if you wish for a stronger flavor.

DIRECTIONS

Cheesecake:

→ Set the oven to 400 degrees.

→ Prepare the apples. Something to consider: this is going to be your serving dish for the cheesecake so you want to keep this looking good. Slice the tops off the apples and hollow out the apples by using either a paring knife or a melon baller to remove the flesh and core. Pay special attention to not damage the sides or the bottom. Eat the apple flesh that you have removed; it's good for you. If the apple does not sit flat in the pan, shave a bit off the bottom of the apple.

→ Place the apples, bottom side down, in a shallow baking pan. In a small sauce pan, melt the butter on medium heat, and stir in the brown sugar and cinnamon. Brush the butter mixture on the inside and top of the apple. Cook the apples for 10 minutes, remove from the oven, and set aside. Lower the oven to 300 degrees.

→ In a standing mixture, add the cream cheese and beat until light and fluffy. Add the sugar, and mix well. Add each egg, one at a time, scraping the sides and the bottom of the bowl between each egg. Beat until you do not see any lumps. Finish off with the vanilla paste, stir, and turn the mixer off.

→ Add 2 heaping tsp crushed graham crackers to the bottom of each cooled apple. You will have some graham crackers left over—save them as a garnish when you serve the dessert.

- Add the cheesecake batter to each apple. Do not over fill, stopping just before the top of the apple, as the batter will rise when cooking.

- Add the apples to a baking pan, and cook for 40 minutes. Remove from the oven and let cool. Store in the refrigerator, covered, for at least 4 hours. It's better if you do this overnight.

Bourbon Caramel Sauce:

- Meanwhile, make the caramel. Prepare your ingredients beforehand as this moves quickly.

- In a heavy saucepan on medium heat, add the sugar. Let it sit and do not stir it, but do not go anywhere either. You will start to see the sides of the sugar starting to brown and smoke. Again, do not stir and do not panic; just turn on the fan. Once the sugar begins to turn an amber color, gentle swirl the pan. Let me say this, and trust me you won't need to be told this twice: melted sugar is *hot* and hurts for at least a few days if you get the sugar on your skin or tongue (I just could not wait). Using a wooden spoon, stir the sugar. Be prepared for the melted sugar to spit and boil a bit.

- Now, add the butter, 2 pats at a time. As the pats melt, add another 2 pats. Stir the mixture the entire time. Once the butter has melted and the caramel is starting to come together, turn the heat off, and remove the pan from the burner.

- While stirring, slowly drizzle in the cream. Once all the cream is in the pan, put the pan back on the burner, and set it to medium heat. Stir until it begins to boil, and the mixture is creamy. Add the bourbon and salt. Stir, remove from the heat, and set aside. Pour the caramel in a pretty container and store in the refrigerator for a few hours until it thickens.

- Time to serve the dessert! Add a nice big dollop of caramel to the plate, and place the apple on top. Sprinkle with the remaining graham crackers and a light dusting of cinnamon.

Fish House Punch

"One of sour, two of sweet, three of strong, four of weak." —Barbadian national rhyme

Although the name itself does not sound appealing (we really don't want to drink anything that has the word fish *in the name), this very strong concoction hails from a fishing club in Philadelphia. It was first served in 1732, and the first record of its ingredients was published in 1744.*

INGREDIENTS

½ cup sugar
1¾ cups water
¾ cup fresh lemon juice
375 ml amber rum
6 oz cognac
1 oz peach brandy
Ice

To Make Mixed Drink:
2 cups premade half ice tea and half lemonade

Rumor has it that George Washington raised a glass thirteen times to toast all thirteen colonies and did not recover for three days (thirteen days would've made a funnier story). We feel your pain, George. Oh, do we feel your pain.

DIRECTIONS

↠ Mix sugar and water. Stir until sugar is dissolved.

↠ Add lemon juice, rum, cognac, peach brandy, and sugar water into an airtight container. Seal and store mixture in the refrigerator for at least 24 hours. The alcohol flavor of the Fish House Punch will soften the longer it is stored.

↠ You can serve this two ways: on the rocks or as a mixed drink. To make the mixed drink, combine in a blender ½ cup Fish House Punch, 1 cup ice, and 2 cups premade half ice tea and half lemonade mixture. Blend briefly until ice is crushed. The mixture will briefly develop foam on top, but it will quickly go away, leaving a drink that tastes like ice tea without an alcohol flavor.

↠ This is deceivingly good. This portion serves two. However, double or triple the batch to serve a big group of friends, but maybe do not raise your glass thirteen times; once or twice should suffice.

Where Are My Olives?

A VERY BRIEF HISTORY OF THE SPANISH SETTLEMENT IN THE NEW WORLD

When the Spanish arrived in the New World, they were shocked and horrified at the available foods. Spain was a nation of clear class distinctions and extremely stubborn beliefs in what was considered "proper food." Reports were sent back to the homeland that there just wasn't enough Spanish food, so great effort was put into establishing crops that suited their particular tastes. Since the Spanish settled in areas such as Florida and New Mexico, their European crops did well in these climates. They certainly made some adaptations, and after working with the indigenous people from these areas, they eventually discovered a few modern favorites . . .

LET THEM EAT (LITTLE) CAKE!

One of the most popular discoveries in the New World was what the Spanish settlers called *tortillas* (which translates to *little cake*). Yup, that's right, tortillas! These flat, round disks of dough were the primary food source of the Aztecs (and had been since about 3000 BC). Maize pancakes for everyone! The Spanish colonists were won over by this new bread, and exciting culinary collaborations emerged. Culture and opinions were shifting and colliding. The settlers enjoyed the new flavors, filling and dipping their pancakes with spices and game.

CUCKOO FOR COCOA

The cocoa bean was used as a form of currency and also to flavor water (along with hot chilies) by the Aztecs and Mayans. It was a sacred crop dating back thousands of years. During one of his visits, Christopher Columbus collected and brought back the beans to Spain. The concept of drinking cocoa took off and soon became quite popular with Spanish nobility, with some minor modifications. The Spanish palate did not favor the bitter cocoa taste, so sugar was added.

chipotle, Cinnamon, and Chocolate Pot de Crème, Olé!

The pepper is ever so subtle in flavor, and it complements the cinnamon and chocolate.

INGREDIENTS

2 cups heavy cream
½ cup whole milk
2 cinnamon sticks
1 dried chipotle pepper, whole
6 oz bittersweet or semisweet chocolate, chopped
½ cup sugar
6 large egg yolks

Optional:
Fresh whipped cream
Sprinkle of cinnamon powder

DIRECTIONS

➔ In a deep saucepan, add the cream, milk, cinnamon sticks, and pepper. Allow to simmer on medium-low for 20 minutes. Remove from heat and let cool slightly. Cover with foil and allow steeping in refrigerator for 3 hours.

➔ Remove the chilled cream from the refrigerator. Discard the pepper and cinnamon. Place the pan back on the stovetop and set the heat to medium. Once the cream warms (do not boil), remove from heat. Stir in the chocolate using a whisk, continuing to stir until the chocolate has melted and is fully incorporated.

➔ In a separate bowl, combine the sugar and egg yolks. Slowly—and we mean snail slow—add the hot chocolate mixture into the sugar and eggs, whisking the entire time. Once everything has been mixed together, prepare a strainer over a bowl. Strain the mixture and discard any lumps (or cooked lumps of eggs . . . if you were a little heavy-handed with the hot mixture).

➔ Set oven to 325 degrees. Pour the mixture into 4 ramekins, and cover with aluminum foil.

➔ Prepare a bain-marie, which is a fancy way of saying set the ramekins in a larger pan that has been filled with water—this allows for slow and gentle cooking of delicate dishes. The water level in the pan should be halfway up the sides of the ramekins. Set the pan in the oven on the center rack, and cook until you find that the sides of the custard are firm and the center jiggles slightly.

➔ We used a larger ramekin, and cooking time was 1 hour 45 minutes. You may need to adjust the time depending on the size of your ramekin. Remember, there is a lot of cream to cook at a low temperature, so this not a 45-minute-and-done dish. Low and slow to let it shine!

➔ Optional: serve with a dollop of whipped cream and a sprinkle of cinnamon. Your guests will give you two thumbs up!

Native Americans

There were many different tribes of Native Americans throughout the New World, and each had their own way of preparing foods, depending on which part of the country they called home. Corn was clearly their main ingredient. Corn was eaten ripe, dried, boiled and dried, soaked and boiled, and pounded into flour. This corn flour was used to thicken soups or make dumplings. Beans were also very prominent in the Native American diet. They too were boiled, dried, pounded, etc.

Also on the Native American menu were venison, elk, buffalo, raccoons, rabbits, oysters, clams, and all game and fish available. The indigenous people used bear fat in place of lard or butter and developed all sorts of cooking techniques that involved boiling, roasting, and baking. They were brilliant farmers and hunters, doing both on a seasonal cycle. They made wine from corn and fruit and used acorns and roots in their dishes. Along the coast, tribes would gather oysters, clams, scallops, and eels.

Sapaen (a name given by the Dutch) was a dish that was made from pounded corn mush cooked with dried meat or fish. This was often served to visitors and guests.

Flavor came from animal fat, as well as ground nuts, wild herbs, and even water lilies—the bulb of the lily was boiled to infuse a dish with flavor. Water lilies were often referred to as an Indian turnip. Meats were cooked on skewers or by placing them on a wood slab above the fire.

Boiled Strawberry Bread

Okay, it's not boiled; we cheated.

INGREDIENTS

½ stick unsalted butter, room temperature (plus extra to grease)
3 cups all-purpose flour (plus extra to dust)
2 tsp baking powder
½ tsp salt
1½ cups sugar
¾ cup canola oil
2 large eggs
1 tsp vanilla paste
1 cup buttermilk
3 cups strawberries, hulled and chopped

DIRECTIONS

⇥ Set oven at 350 degrees. Grease an 8x8 square pan with butter and dust with flour; set aside.

⇥ In a bowl, combine flour, baking powder, and salt; set aside.

⇥ In a mixing bowl, whip butter. When light and fluffy, add sugar, followed by oil. Once the ingredients are combined, add the eggs, one at a time. Finish this step by adding the vanilla.

⇥ Now you are going to alternate the next ingredients in three cycles. While the mixer is going, add a third of the dry mixture, followed by a third of the buttermilk. Repeat two more times. You may need to stop the mixer and scrape down the sides, and do not forget about the bottom of the mixing bowl, as heavier ingredients sometimes get stuck at the bottom and do not mix fully.

⇥ Now that the ingredients have made a heavy batter, turn the mixer off and fold the strawberries into the batter.

⇥ Pour the finished batter into the prepared pan. Cook for 55 minutes to 1 hour.

Corn Cakes

Light, delicate, and delectable.

INGREDIENTS

2 Tbsp unsalted butter, divided
1 onion, diced (we used a sweet onion)
2 cups corn (if you are using frozen corn,
   completely thaw and drain)
2 eggs, beaten
1 tsp salt
¼ tsp white pepper
5 Tbsp self-rising flour
1 tsp fresh chives, minced

DIRECTIONS

→ Melt ½ Tbsp butter on medium heat in a fry
  pan. Add the onion and sauté until softened
  but do not brown.

→ In a medium sized mixing bowl, combine
  cooked onion, corn, eggs, salt, white pepper,
  flour, and chives.

→ In a large fry pan on medium heat, melt
  remaining 1½ Tbsp butter. Drop a spoonful
  of corn cake mixture onto the fry pan. Using
  the back of the spoon, slightly flatten and
  shape the corn cake. Repeat, but do not
  crowd the pan. Lightly brown all sides of the
  corn cakes, remove from the pan, and place
  on paper towels.

→ Serve alone, or as a base to our Praise Be
  to Cod with applejack coulis (page 98).

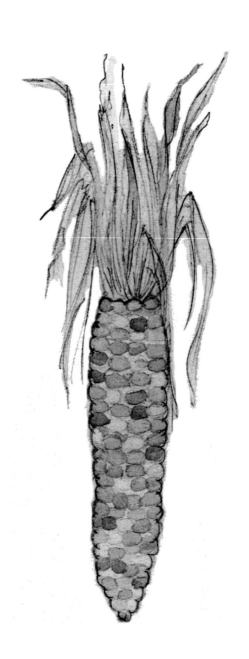

Seafood Stew

Do not try to be polite—just dig in and get messy.

INGREDIENTS

8 Tbsp unsalted butter
2 sweet medium onions, diced
3 cloves garlic, minced
1 sweet potato, peeled and diced small
1 parsnip, peeled and diced small
2 carrots, peeled and diced small
½ cup all-purpose flour
6 cups seafood stock
1⅛ tsp salt
1 tsp pepper
1½ tsp ground coriander
4 cups green cabbage, roughly chopped
1 tsp fresh thyme, leaves removed from stem
½ lb chopped clams, plus the juice from the clams
½ lb haddock, cut into bite-size pieces
½ lb cod, cut into bite-size pieces
½ lb scallops (depending on the size of your scallops, you may want to cut into quarters. We use the size U10.)

DIRECTIONS

→ Melt the butter in a Dutch oven over medium-low heat. Add the onions and garlic and cook until they start to soften, then follow with the potatoes, parsnips, and carrots. Stir occasionally and cook for about 15 minutes, or until the vegetables are barely cooked.

→ Add the flour and reduce the temperature to medium-low. Cook for around 3 minutes, while stirring. The flour will coat the vegetables and start to cook in the pan.

→ Slowly add the seafood stock to the pan, stirring to prevent lumps, along with the salt, pepper, coriander, cabbage, and thyme. Raise the heat to medium-high until the stock begins to boil. Drop the heat down to a simmer and add the remaining seafood.

→ Cook for 15 minutes on simmer, and the soup will be ready.

→ Though you can certainly eat it immediately, this soup tastes better after the flavors have had time to incorporate. Keep that in mind as you plan your meal.

Brûléed Indian Pudding

A uniquely American dish with a modern topping. Depending on the size of your ramekins, this should make about 6 individual desserts.

INGREDIENTS

1 cup whole milk
3 cups heavy cream
1 tsp ground ginger
½ tsp nutmeg
1 tsp cinnamon
Pinch cloves
½ cup cornmeal
2 Tbsp unsalted butter
1 cup dark molasses
3 eggs, whisked
½ cup sugar
Whipped cream (optional)

DIRECTIONS

⇥ Set oven to 300 degrees. With the heat off, add the milk, cream, ginger, nutmeg, cinnamon, and cloves to a saucepan. Sprinkle cornmeal while stirring. This assists with keeping the cornmeal from getting lumpy.

⇥ Turn the heat on to medium, and add butter. Stir frequently until thickened—the back of the spoon will be coated. You may need to adjust the heat to a lower temperature as the mixture thickens to avoid burning.

⇥ On medium-low heat, continue to cook the pudding and add molasses. Stir until

fully incorporated, then turn the heat off. Let the mixture cool. This is a very important step; if you do not allow your pudding to cool, your eggs will cook. Once cooled, slowly add eggs while stirring.

⇥ Add mixture to ramekins, and place on a baking pan to prevent any spillage in your oven. Cook for 1 hour. Remove from heat, cool, and place in the refrigerator to chill.

⇥ Place a Silpat-lined cookie sheet on a flat surface, near your stove. In a heavy saucepan, add sugar and heat on medium heat. Do not stir (even if you want to). You might want to turn your kitchen fan on. As the sugar begins to dissolve, it will start to turn the color of amber. Swirl the pan a bit until it dissolves all the sugar. Once the sugar is fully dissolved, give it a quick stir with a wooden spoon. Turn the heat off, and evenly spread the caramelized sugar over the silpat. You might want to gently tilt the pan to spread the hot mixture. Set this aside until it is fully cooled.

⇥ Using your hands, break up the sugar into chunks. Add the hard sugar chunks to a food processor and pulse until it becomes a powder.

⇥ Turn the oven on to low broil. Lightly sprinkle the magical sugar dust over the cooled pudding. Again, place the ramekins on a baking pan and set in the oven for just a few minutes. The sugar dust will turn to liquid and become shiny. Remove from the oven, and cool slightly before serving.

⇥ Clink! Break the sugar coating and enjoy. You can make these a day or two in advance. Serve with a dollop of lightly sweetened whipped cream (optional).

Union Oyster House

Rich history, delicious oysters.

If you have ever been to Boston, it is more than likely that you have been told to stop in at the Union Oyster House. And if you haven't been, we highly recommend a trip. Be sure to ask for Jimmy the bar manager—he knows quite a bit about the history, the building, and all the famous celebrities who have dined within those walls.

The building, located at 41 Union Street, has been a landmark for over 250 years. In 1771, it was the home of the oldest newspaper in the United States, *The Massachusetts Spy*, where publisher Isaiah Thomas printed news and information leading to the Revolution.

In 1796, the future King of France Louis Phillippe spent his years of exile living on the second floor while teaching French to the more fashionable ladies of Boston.

During this time (early 1800s), the oyster craze became a hot trend. Almost every city had oyster parlors, oyster cellars, and oyster salons that popped up on main streets.

It was in 1826 that Atwood & Bacon opened up the oyster bar. The original semicircular raw bar is still in place (we know because we recently sat there ourselves, devouring everything they could shuck). Frequent customers included Daniel Webster (who drank brandy and water with each six plates of oysters he ate), Paul Revere, and in more modern times the entire Kennedy clan. Booth 18 is still dedicated to the late John F. Kennedy.

Original menu items included oysters from Virginia, Narragansett, Cape Cod, and Ipswich, as well as little necks, quahogs, scallops, dry toast, buttered toast, fried eggs, and several pies.

The Union Oyster House has had only three owners since 1826.

FUN FACT

The toothpick was first used at the Union Oyster House. Charles Forster of Maine imported them from South America and hired Harvard boys to dine there and ask for toothpicks as part of his clever marketing campaign. Clearly it worked.

chowdahhhh

That's how we say "chowder" in Massachusetts. Our take on a traditional New England favorite (this is not the Union Oyster House recipe; that's a secret). As with any soup, it is delicious at the time it is made, but always much better the next day.

INGREDIENTS

½ lb bacon, cut into ½-inch pieces*
¼ cup water
3 Tbsp unsalted butter
1 clove garlic, minced
1 medium onion (about 1½ cups), finely chopped
2 stalks celery (about 1½ cups), finely chopped
8 oz clam juice
3 cups whole milk
1 cup light cream
2 bay leaves
Salt, to taste
Pepper, to taste
24 oz baby Yukon Gold potatoes, skin on
12 live cherrystone clams
16 oz chopped clams in juice
1 cup heavy cream

*TIP

We like the smokiness of bacon, but if you do not care for the taste, you can replace it with salt pork.

DIRECTIONS

→ Combine bacon and water in a Dutch oven over medium heat, stirring occasionally, until water has evaporated and bacon has begun to brown and crisp in spots, about 8 minutes. Add butter, garlic, onions, and celery. Continue to cook, stirring occasionally, until onions are softened but not browned, about 4 minutes longer.

→ Add clam juice, and stir to combine. Add milk, light cream, bay leaves, and salt and pepper to taste. Increase the heat to medium-high.

→ Now, prepare the potatoes. Separate 6 potatoes to the side; dice the remaining potatoes to your liking. We like when the potatoes are diced into small, bite-size pieces. The 6 separated potatoes should simply be cut in half. Add all the potatoes to the Dutch oven.

→ Once the milk boils, add the 12 live clams, laying them flat. Reduce the heat to medium, and cover. Once the clams open, gently remove them from the pot as you want to keep the clams in the shell. As you remove the clams, tilt them slightly until the liquid inside flows back into the pan. Set the clams aside to cool. Once the clam shells are cool enough to touch, remove the whole clams, chop, and set aside. At this point, do not worry if the chowder consistency begins to break (this means you can see the fat from the butter and milk separate from the juice). It is going to get nice and smooth after the next step.

✴ Remove the bay leaves. With a slotted spoon, remove the 6 potatoes that have been halved from the chowder. They should be tender and smell really good. Place the potatoes in the blender, along with 1 cup of liquid from the hot chowder. Puree the potatoes on high speed until they are smooth and emulsified, about 2 minutes. Return the puree back to the chowder in Dutch oven. Stir.

✴ Add the clams that were cooked in the shells and the chopped clams (and their juice) to the chowder. Now, slowly add the heavy cream, and stir to combine. Reheat until the chowder is simmering. Season well with salt and pepper.

COLONIAL COCKTAILS

Spruce Beer
Spruce was first used by settlers to flavor tea; later, it was used to flavor ship-brewed beer.

Cock Ale
This brew was first popular in England and made its way across the pond. It was a simple ale flavored with cock broth.

Quince Wine
The colonists made many different wines flavored with various fruits found in the New World, including quince, which tastes similar to a pear.

Rattle-Skull
The term "rattle-skull" refers to an overly chatty person; the drink, however, is a blend of dark beer, rum, lime juice, and nutmeg.

Flip
A delicate mixture of beer, rum, sugar, and eggs. Thomas Jefferson had at least a dozen recipes for various flips, including a "Sleeper Flip" that combined aged rum, sugar, egg, cloves, lemon, and coriander.

Hard Apple Cider
Colonists began growing cider apples as early as 1623. Apple crops were very successful, so the beverage was always available.

Whiskey
In the 1700s, whiskey was once used as currency during the American Revolution. American whiskey is fermented with a mash of grains.

Kentucky Bourbon
Barrel-aged and made from corn, the birth of Kentucky bourbon goes back to the 1770s when Kentucky was still considered Virginia. Batches were sent out in oak barrels and stamped as being from Bourbon County.

Fish House Punch
A rum-based beverage, made with cognac and peach brandy. Fish House Punch was first served in Philadelphia around 1732.

Sources

Booth, Sally Smith. *Hung, Strung & Potted*. New York: Clarkson N. Potter, Inc., 1971.

Bullock, Mrs. Helen. *The Williamsburg Art of Cookery or Accomplis'd Gentlewoman's Companion*. Richmond, VA: Colonial Williamsburg, 1966.

Carter, Susannah. *The Frugal Colonial Housewife*. Garden City, NY: Dolphin Books, 1976.

Dooley, Don. *The Better Homes & Gardens Heritage Cook Book*. New York: Meredith Corporation, 1975.

Glasse, Hannah. *The Art of Cookery, Made Plain and Easy*. Mineola, NY: Dover Publications, 2015.

Grasse, Steven. *Colonial Spirits: A Toast to Our Drunken History*. New York: Abrams Image, 2016.

Hirsch, Corin. *Forgotten Drinks of Colonial New England*. Charleston, SC: American Palate, 2014.

Langseth-Christensen, Lillian. *The Mystic Seaport Cookbook*. Secaucus, NJ: The Marine Historical Association, 1970.

Oliver, Sandra L. *Food in Colonial and Federal America*. Westport, CT: Greenwood Press, 2005.

O'Neill Grace, Catherine, and Margaret M. Bruchac with Plimoth Plantation. 1621: *A New Look at Thanksgiving*. Washington, DC: National Geographic, 2001.

Plymouth Antiquarian Society. *The Plimoth Colony Cook Book*. Mineola, NY: Dover Publications, 2005.

Russell, Howard S. *Indian New England Before the Mayflower.* Lebanon, NH: University Press of New England, 1980.

Simmons, Amelia. *The First American Cookbook, A Facsimile of "American Cookery," 1796.* New York: Dover Publications, Inc., 1958.

Smith, Eliza. *The Compleat Housewife.* Kansas City, MO: American Antiquarian Society, 2012.

Taylor, Dale. *The Writer's Guide to Everyday Life in Colonial America.* Cincinnati, OH: Writer's Digest Book, 1997.

About the Authors

Lisa Graves

Author and illustrator Lisa Graves grew up in the small, historic town of Millis, Massachusetts, where she explored her love of drawing and history at an early age in her father's sign shop.

In 2010, after fifteen years spent illustrating for corporate and retail clients, she combined her passion for art and history once again by launching *History Witch*, a weekly series dedicated to fascinating stories and portraits of women.

Her artwork drew the attention of Xist Publishing, with whom she developed the "Women in History" series of elementary school books for girls, and Skyhorse Publishing, which has published several of her books collaborating with women authors, including Dr. Lois Frankel's *Ageless Women, Timeless Wisdom*.

Lisa was commissioned to design and illustrate the cover of *Salem Haunted Happenings* and gives lectures and workshops across New England. She has been a contributor to *Young Vagabond* and *New Moon* magazines. She lives in Medway with her family in a home built in 1852.

Tricia Cohen

Food lover and recipe creator Tricia Cohen grew up in the town of Plainville, Massachusetts, on a street where neighbors were considered relatives and her family welcomed people with fresh, homemade foods.

Her family's house, filled with love and laughter, had two kitchens—one for her grandmother and one for her parents. Friends and family who gathered to share meals knew they would find good conversation and tasty recipes made from organic produce harvested from the garden her grandfather lovingly tended.

In her own home, Tricia continues to share the love of family and food as a skilled hostess and gourmet cook. She teaches others the traditions she learned and engages her guests with culinary art, using fresh, local produce and interesting spices.

Tricia sharpens her craft by reading cookbooks, attending cooking classes, and occasionally assisting an acclaimed professional chef as a sous-chef.

She and her husband, Michael, live with their four dogs in Pittsburgh, Pennsylvania, and North Truro, Massachusetts.

Conversion Charts

METRIC AND IMPERIAL CONVERSIONS
(These conversions are rounded for convenience)

Ingredient	Cups/Tablespoons/Teaspoons	Ounces	Grams/Milliliters
Butter	1 cup = 16 tablespoons = 2 sticks	8 ounces	230 grams
Cheese, shredded	1 cup	4 ounces	110 grams
Cream cheese	1 tablespoon	0.5 ounce	14.5 grams
Cornstarch	1 tablespoon	0.3 ounce	8 grams
Flour, all-purpose	1 cup/1 tablespoon	4.5 ounces/0.3 ounce	125 grams/8 grams
Flour, whole wheat	1 cup	4 ounces	120 grams
Fruit, dried	1 cup	4 ounces	120 grams
Fruits or veggies, chopped	1 cup	5 to 7 ounces	145 to 200 grams
Fruits or veggies, puréed	1 cup	8.5 ounces	245 grams
Honey, maple syrup, or corn syrup	1 tablespoon	.75 ounce	20 grams
Liquids: cream, milk, water, or juice	1 cup	8 fluid ounces	240 milliliters
Oats	1 cup	5.5 ounces	150 grams
Salt	1 teaspoon	0.2 ounce	6 grams
Spices: cinnamon, cloves, ginger, or nutmeg (ground)	1 teaspoon	0.2 ounce	5 milliliters
Sugar, brown, firmly packed	1 cup	7 ounces	200 grams
Sugar, white	1 cup/1 tablespoon	7 ounces/0.5 ounce	200 grams/12.5 grams
Vanilla extract	1 teaspoon	0.2 ounce	4 grams

OVEN TEMPERATURES

Fahrenheit	Celsius	Gas Mark
225°	110°	¼
250°	120°	½
275°	140°	1
300°	150°	2
325°	160°	3
350°	180°	4
375°	190°	5
400°	200°	6
425°	220°	7
450°	230°	8

Index